HEAT

D1029422

EAST HEATH

Site of
Old Hampstead
Spa

CHURCH WALK
WELL HILL
①

Site of
Elm Cottage
④

DOWNSHIRE HILL
JOHN STREET

REET

ROSSLYN
HILL
②
Wentworth
Place

POND STREET

SOUTH END
GREEN

HAVERSTOCK HILL

KEY

1 Where house of Bentley the postman, was
   and the Keats brothers lived in 1817-18

2 Residence of Dilke and Brown, built
   1815, where Keats lived after 1st Dec 1818

3 Location of Leigh Hunt's cottage

4 Location of Mrs Brawne's residence 1818

5 Where Keats took coach to London

BELSIZE LANE

ondon

To London

LIBRARY

TALLAHASSEE

FLORIDA

THE SPIRIT OF PLACE IN KEATS

The beautiful façade of John Clarke's school at Enfield
John Keats attended this school from 1803 to 1811

GUY MURCHIE

THE SPIRIT OF PLACE
IN KEATS

Sketches of persons and places
known by him, and his
reaction to them

WITH A FOREWORD BY
THE ASSISTANT CURATOR AND LIBRARIAN
OF THE KEATS MEMORIAL HOUSE
HAMPSTEAD

NEWMAN NEAME LIMITED

PR
4836
M7
1955

First published in 1955 by
NEWMAN NEAME LIMITED
50 Fitzroy Street London W1
Copyright 1955 by Guy Murchie
All rights reserved

Printed in Great Britain by
THE MILLBROOK PRESS
Southampton

828
K257ma

LIBRARY
FLORIDA STATE UNIVERSITY
TALLAHASSEE, FLORIDA

TO MY WIFE

294437

CONTENTS

LIST OF ILLUSTRATIONS

ERRATUM

The plate facing page 16 shows
the parish church of St Andrew at Enfield

FOREWORD

BY J. H. PRESTON

ASSISTANT CURATOR AND LIBRARIAN
OF KEATS HOUSE HAMPSTEAD

OVER THIRTY YEARS AGO Thomas Hardy visited the
Hampstead home of John Keats. He felt impelled to
write a tribute in honour of his fellow poet, who like
himself was of West Country extraction. Hardy, one
of the first of the pilgrims who have since come in
their thousands to this house, sensed the living presence of the man Keats, young and unfamed in his
day. Shelley had said his friend would never die, but
would live with the Immortals. 'Come you haunting
here,' wrote Hardy 'where streets have grown up all
around?'

So we, later votaries, praise the fame of this Keats.
Praise it not only because of the excellence and greatness of a life's work, but also because to us, even as to
Shelley and Hardy, the realisation of his immortality
has dawned.

The author of *The Spirit of Place in Keats* is surely
one of these votaries. He began, while in college, by
buying the life mask of Keats and has continued to
read the letters and poems and to explore the haunts
of the poet ever since.

Often for him a visit to England has meant a tour of the 'Keats country'. To trace the beginnings where the plaque in Moorgate Street, London marks the site of the 'livery and bait' establishment where Keats was born, son of the chief ostler who later became proprietor. Then to journey to north-east London where the River Lea runs through the rapidly urbanising countryside and to find the railway station standing on the site of Mr Clarke's school at Enfield. Then to see the plaque which marks where the young doctor-poet's cottage stood in Keats Parade, Edmonton. One is glad to find that this site of early inspiration has been recognised and named in honour of one who lived there.

It is a long pilgrimage; Keats observed and wrote far afield. Teignmouth, the Isle of Wight, Winchester, Chichester, Burford Bridge, Bedhampton and even over the Solway Firth into the country of Burns, Scott and Keats's Meg the Gypsy, where he and Brown, as weather beaten and shabby as gypsies themselves braved the stings of gadflies and the rigours of Scottish weather.

All these delights and more are experienced before the culmination at Hampstead where Keats, in happy mood, 'stood tip-toe on a little hill' enjoying the sweet air of the village which was to be his home. And so to Wentworth Place, his house in the quiet garden where one absorbs the academic peace of the surroundings.

His parlour with the chairs in position as if he still sat there, his arm resting on the back of another chair 'like the picture of somebody reading' is surely the place where his spirit lives most strongly. In this house are his books, his homely relics and those of his 'fair love' Fanny Brawne. On the sofa in front of the window facing the old mulberry tree the poet seems still to sit to watch the ordinary everyday happenings going on around the house.

One may walk across to the little house in Kentish Town, the home of Leigh Hunt where Keats stayed for a while, and see also the cottage in Wesleyan Place, Keats's lodging for a few days before he returned to Wentworth Place, ill and desponding, to be cared for by Fanny Brawne and her mother during his last month in England before he boarded the *Maria Crowther* en route for Naples and the Piazza di Spagna, Rome.

And the tomb in the protestant cemetery? A name that is 'writ in water'? Surely the most unhappy epitaph a man ever had, but as surely as Shelley was the first to reverse its verdict, so time and posterity have proved its reversal true and shown that Adonais is not dead.

'The soul of Adonais like a star
Beacons from the abode where the Eternal are.'
             J. H. PRESTON
        (author of *The Story of Hampstead* etc)

PREFACE

THE UNFOLDING of events in John Keats's life and his development have an interest equal to that of his great verse. Many persons familiar with his poetry know little of his life except it was short and peppered with adversity. To be a great man, as Keats proved himself to be, required a certain quality over and above pre-eminent ability in a particular business or talent.

It has been said that good biography should be of three parts: the life story, the portrait and the message. Keats painted his own portrait in his letters; and his message, often repeated, was: 'I am certain of nothing but the holiness of the Heart's affections and the truth of Imagination – what the imagination seizes as Beauty must be truth – whether it existed before or not' – to which he added:

> *A thing of beauty is a joy for ever:*
> *Its loveliness increases; it will never*
> *Pass into nothingness;*

Now a truism but original with Keats.

Although endowed with imagination that enabled him to sublimate actual or longed for experience into perfect poetry, he was an objective thinker, intensely aware of concrete realities. His dauntless courage, friendliness, humility, generosity, manliness, upright character and native philosophy were qualities, as much as his genius, that made him the man he was.

I believe *influence of place* had a marked effect on the writings of Keats for 'places reflect the natures they arouse.' The Middlesex countryside, London, Hampstead, Teignmouth, Chichester, Bedhampton and Winchester fired his imagination. Critical study of literary sources of his poems has not been attempted. On the other hand I have discussed the places and events that effected his genius and brought him success in his earnest effort to leave to posterity a worthwhile legacy.

So long as his health remained, Keats was master of his emotions. Idealisation of poetry as an art and a thing of beauty controlled the quest for love. Disease gradually put out his fires, leaving ashes of discontent and unhappiness. The starry attributes now attached to his name appeared above the horizon only after his death, belatedly seeking to catch up with him in his flight across the sky.

In but one of his many letters did John ever mention his parents and then only to say that he sealed his letters with their intertwined initials. He made his way in life without any help from them except through one fateful decision. To them he owed his good fortune in being placed at the budding age of eight in a good school in an historic English county where he was given free opportunity to absorb classical history, romantic poetry and legends and at the same time live in a countryside full of birds, flowers and other natural objects.

Willa Cather, a distinguished author herself, has maintained that 'the years from eight to fifteen are the formative period of a writer's life when he unconsciously gathers basic material. He may acquire a great many interesting and vivid impressions in his mature years but his thematic material he acquires under fifteen years of age. Other writers will tell you this. Lord Dunsany once told me that he believed he had never used any basic material he had acquired after his fifteenth year.' This remarkable statement seems to fit the development of John Keats who spent those years in Middlesex at the school of John Clarke.

G.M.

ACKNOWLEDGMENTS

I AM GRATEFUL to Mr J. H. Preston, Assistant Curator of Keats House, for his graceful Foreword. It is a summary of the intent of my book. Supplementing my own efforts at research I am indebted for brief quotations from their writings on the life of John Keats to H. Buxton Forman, Sir Sidney Colvin, H. W. Garrod, Amy Lowell, Dorothy Hewlitt, William Sharp and others.

My attention was first called to the Old Mill House at Bedhampton through the kindness of F. R. Byerley of Bedhampton, but the positive identification and description of the famous house as the exact place of the poet's visits was made possible by the co-operation and hospitality of Captain and Mrs B. R. Willett who now occupy the house.

For their kindness in reading my first draft and for their encouragement I am grateful to Arthur S. Pier of Boston, Charles F. Todd of New Brunswick, Mrs Wilmot Matthews of Toronto, Miss Jane Boulanger of London, and to Buchanan Charles of North Andover, Massachusetts. To the latter I am under a special debt for many happy changes in phrasing made at his suggestion.

I wish to express my appreciation of the courtesy extended to me by the following holders of copyrights in granting permission to quote from publications under their control: Alfred A. Knopf, New York for a sentence taken from the Preface to E. K. Brown's *Willa Cather: A Critical Biography;* Yale University Press, New Haven, for the poem entitled *The Name Writ in Water* from Robert Underwood Johnson's *Collected Poems,* and for quotations from George H. Ford's *Keats and the Victorians;* Harpers & Brothers for a stanza beginning 'My heart being hungry feeds on food' from Edna St Vincent Millay's *The Harp Weaver and Other Poems;* Faber & Faber Ltd, London, for a quotation about Keats's letters from T. S. Eliot's *The Use of Poetry and the Use of Criticism;* Oxford University Press, for a short extract from H. W. Garrod's Oxford University lecture on Keats; and to William Heineman Ltd, London, for quotations from *John Keats: The Living Year* by Robert Gittings.

It is a pleasure to concede my indebtedness to Walter Muir Whitehill, Director of the Boston Athenaeum, and his efficient staff for their interest and cooperation, and to Ralph W. Langley who drew the endpapers.

CHAPTER ONE

MIDDLESEX: 1803-15

AT THE BEGINNING of the nineteenth century London was a pygmy compared with Metropolitan London of today. Clinging to its main thoroughfare, the River Thames, it had stretched only from east to west. Thomas de Quincey has told in his *Confessions of an Opium Eater* how accessible then lay the open country to the north. He often wandered on moonlight nights along Oxford Street, he said, 'gazing up every avenue in succession which pierces through the heart of Marylebone to the fields and woods, travelling with my eyes up the long vistas which lay part in light and part in shade; that is, said I, the road to the north'.

Taking this road to the north in 1803, one would have come upon two small villages, Enfield and Edmonton, nestled in the woods of Middlesex, ten miles from London. They were important places in the development of John Keats as man and poet. He spent in and around these villages at the home of his grandparents in Ponders End or Edmonton, at John Clarke's school in Enfield, and finally at Edmonton as surgeon's apprentice to Thomas Hammond, the first twenty years of his short life.

Middlesex County had a romantic history in its early days and in Keats's time its natural beauty had

B

not been encroached on by the expansion of London. It was then a fit nursery for the growth of imagination in a romantic poet.

King Harold founded ancient Waltham Abbey by the River Lea on the border of Middlesex. There he prayed in vain for victory over the Normans before the Battle of Hastings in 1066. When his slain body was carried there after the battle, it became his shrine.

In Plantagenet days the Royal Progress bearing the remains of Eleanor, queen of Edward I, passed near Enfield. Its halting place four miles from Enfield is still marked by Waltham Cross. And at Barnet and Hadley on the edge of Enfield Chase two battles were fought in the Wars of the Roses. The fate of Warwick, the king maker, was sealed at Barnet.

Several ancient defensive moats, ready to be explored, existed near Enfield when Keats was at school. People of substance naturally had attempted, by the best manner then known, to safeguard their properties in much fought over Middlesex.

Enfield Manor House, still standing in 1803, was in King Henry VIII's possession at the end of his reign. It adjoined Enfield Chase, a royal hunting preserve of 3,200 acres. Princess Elizabeth was living there when her father died on 28th January 1547. Her brother, Edward VI, then at Hertford, was brought next day to Enfield where he learned of the King's death and held Court until the last day of June when he removed to London. In 1552 Edward settled the Manor of Enfield on his sister, Elizabeth. The so called 'Palace' at Enfield was built or rebuilt for her use. The walls and chimney piece had the initials (E.R.) and the words *benevolentia regis* marked on them.[1] Elizabeth enjoyed hunting. As Queen, she came frequently to pursue the hart. Game from Enfield Chase graced the royal table as late as the days of Charles II and perhaps of the Georges.

The school at Enfield to which John Keats and his brother George were taken by their parents in 1803, was kept by John Clarke. His son, Cowden Clarke, tutor and close friend of Keats, has given the only first hand description of the school.

The school had been built by a West India merchant about the end of the seventeenth century. It was of the better character of domestic architecture of the period . . . Its design and perfect finish were enough to protect it from destruction when the railroad came to Enfield . . .

In this schoolhouse John Keats all but commenced and did complete his school education . . . He was one of the little fellows who had not actually emerged from the child's costume upon being placed under my Father's care . . .

The house, airy, roomy and substantial, with good allowance of appertaining land, was especially fitted

*for a school. 'The eight-bedded room', and 'six-bed-
ded room', as they were called, give some idea of the
dimensions of the apartments. The school room
which occupied the site which formerly had been
the coach house and stabling, was forty feet long and
the playground was a spacious courtyard between
the school-room and the house . . . From the play-
ground stretched a garden, one hundred yards in
length, where in one corner were some small plots
set aside for certain boys fond of having a garden of
their own that they might cultivate according to
their individual will and pleasure; and farther on
was a sweep of greensward, beyond the centre of
which was a pond, sometimes dignified as 'The
Lake' . . .*

*At the far end of the pond, and in those boyish days
it seemed indeed 'far', beneath the iron railings which
divided our premises from the meadows beyond,
whence the song of the nightingales in May would
reach us in the stillness of night, there stood a rustic
arbour where John Keats and I used to sit and read
Spenser's* Faerie Queene *together, when he had left
school and used to come over from Edmonton where
he was apprenticed to Thomas Hammond the surgeon.*

*On the other side of the house lay a small enclosure
which we called 'the drying ground' and where was
a magnificent old morella cherry tree against a wall
well exposed to the sun. Beyond this a gate led into
a small field or paddock of two acres – the pasture-*

ground of two cows which supplied the establish-
ment with fresh and abundant milk. It was a domain
of almost boundless extent and magnificence to the
imagination of a schoolboy; and it really did possess
solid excellences.

Before John Clarke set up his school at Enfield the
house with its beautiful façade and tracery of carved
brick (now in the South Kensington Museum) was
owned and occupied by Benjamin Disraeli, grandfather of Benjamin Disraeli who became the favourite Prime Minister of Queen Victoria. Old fashioned
Georgian houses, Queen Anne in style, surrounded
the village market. They were mostly of red brick
with gardens and well wooded pleasances. The garden walls had brick posts with balls on top and between the posts open iron railings, wrought in elaborate patterns, so that houses were not entirely shut off.
Along the ridge road and from Trent Park in Enfield
Chase there were wide prospects over Epping Forest
to the Kent hills and across Hertfordshire and Middlesex.

Epping Forest in the valley of the River Lea was
not far from the school and Enfield Chase was actually visible from its windows. These dark woods led
the boys to dwell on the mysteries within them. They
'peopled them with visions,' according to Cowden
Clarke. Dragons and giants, dwarfs and fairies lived
in the woods in the minds of imaginative boys. There

were also birds and flowers in Enfield Chase. A sylvan character remains today in Trent Park where there is a bit of primeval forest called the 'Rough Lot' in which lies a little lake about four acres in extent that finds its way into the River Lea. By this lake and stream of boyhood's memory, Keats may have placed in imagination, 'alone and palely loitering', his famous knight-at-arms.

Along the outlet of Trent Lake the boys from the school collected specimens. Probably this was the spot where John developed his fondness for 'Goldfinches, Tomtits, Minnows, Mice, Ticklebacks, Dace, Cock salmons and all the whole tribe of the Bushes and the Brooks', as he remembered to tell his sister in March 1819. In her old age Fanny Keats Llanos confirmed her brother John's fondness for birds and their joint satisfaction in keeping 'titlebats' and other small fish which he used to gather and store away at their grandmother's house in Edmonton.

There is scarcely a reference to nature or an elaborate simile in all of Keats's writings that may not be traced to the unfading impression made upon his mind in early life. When he began to put his thoughts on paper he found himself recalling the Middlesex woods, flowers, birds and streams as the natural world he loved and knew best His 'I stood tip-toe' is largely Middlesex and so is much of *Sleep and Poetry*. In *Endymion* he told Peona how he used to bubble up water through a reed. In reminiscence he exhorted her:

> *So reaching back to boyhood: make me ships*
> *Of moulted feathers, touchwood, alder chips*
> *With leaves stuck in them; and the Neptune be*
> *Of their petty ocean.*

An instance also of his going back to his youth occurred when Keats, fatally ill, was taken by Leigh Hunt to his house in Kentish Town in June 1820. Hunt was writing, at the time, a piece to be called 'A now-descriptive of a hot day'. Each sentence was to begin with the word *now*. Hunt asked John to suggest some of them. It is interesting to surmise which of the *nows*[2] belong to Keats and are characteristic of him, such as:

Now *grasshoppers 'fry', as Dryden says,*

Now *rooms with the sun on them become intolerable; and the apothecary's apprentice, with a bitterness beyond aloes, thinks of the pond he used to bathe in at school.*

Now *boys assemble around the village Pump with a ladle to it [at Edmonton] and delight to make a forbidden splash and get wet through the shoes.*
Now *also they make suckers of feather and bathe all day long in rivers and ponds and make mighty fishings of 'titlebats.'*

Now *the bee, as he hums along, seems to be talking heavily of the heat.*

Now *a green lane . . . thick set with hedge-row elms, and having a noise of a brook 'rumbling in pebble-stone' is one of the pleasantest things in the world.*

Now *five fat people in a stage coach hate the sixth fat one coming in, and think he has no right to be so large.*

When I visited Enfield I found little resemblance to the unspoiled neighbourhood which existed in the early days of the nineteenth century. The Chase is mostly built over; only Trent Park remains. The pretty country village of Enfield is now a crowded suburb of London. It is fortunate that Cowden Clarke had an impulse to go back to Enfield in 1830 after his father had given up the school and to write an account of his visit, thereby supplying additional details of the atmosphere surrounding school life during the boyhood of Keats.

The old elm in the wide centre place of the town had certainly dwindled. The school-house with the poplars in front has no longer the air of a stately mansion. A noble cedar tree standing in the Palace Garden (Queen Elizabeth's Palace) is reduced to one large branch . . . This cedar was brought from Lebanon in a portmanteau in Queen Anne's reign. There is little doubt, I believe, of Queen Elizabeth having resided here at times on account of the vicinity of the Royal Chase. A bridge northwards from the town still goes by the name of 'The Maiden's Bridge' ... Edward, the boy monarch, was brought to Enfield to be crowned. In this neighbourhood too, not many years since, was still remaining a portion of the building where the conspirators met to watch the motions of King James when he and his Court were at Theobalds [near Enfield] ...

While I was sitting in the window of my inn at sunset, looking at the old house, I heard the old schoolbell ring - the same bell whose appeal I had answered six or seven times a day for an eighth of a century ... To add to the reality, a flock of rooks flew over the play-ground on their way to roost. They must have been the same rooks I used to see every evening of my life; they flew in the same order and there was the same latter-lammas which we used to urge with our raised voices, shouting after him, 'lag, lag, lag'.

Clarke ended his account which was printed in *The Tatler* of 11th October 1830 with a quotation from *Sleep and Poetry* by Keats.

*A laughing school boy without grief or care
Riding the springy branches of an elm.*

Edmonton seems to have fared better in the waste of time than Enfield. It retains in part a village aspect.

Church Street where John's grandmother, Mrs Jennings, and Mr Hammond, the surgeon, lived has an old look with an ancient, square towered church, surrounded by a burial ground and large, fine trees. Evidently, it was a principal street in the early nineteenth century for it contained the post office and municipal offices as well as the old parish church of All Saints and the better residences. Many of the early houses have been torn down to make way for modern buildings. Church Street is now known locally as Keats Parade. It is different but it still remains the street where John as a schoolboy played during vacations, and as apothecary-apprentice, rushed in and out of the little pill-house beside Mr Hammond's mansion. Here it was, too, that he got hit by a snowball while he held the horse of surgeon Hammond making his calls along Church Street.

Opposite the site of Charles Lamb's cottage is a mission house dating from 1784, with the inscription 'A structure of hope founded in Faith on the basis of Charity'. A little blue lady with flowing skirt holds an open book giving her message of cheer from the shelter of a niche just as she did when Keats was a boy. Today, we can see her, as he must often have noticed her, looking down on Keats Parade.

Pymmes brook on its way to the River Lea still flows in some fashion through Edmonton, along which, according to Clarke, schoolboy John used to linger, or

lean on the rail of an old footbridge over the pond on
Edmonton green, to watch

> *Where swarms of minnows show their little heads.*
> *Staying their wavy bodies 'gainst the streams*
> *To taste the luxury of sunny beams*
> *Temper'd with coolness.*

John Clarke, the master of Enfield School has been
described as a man of fine taste in literature, of noble
and liberal opinions, 'as gentle hearted as he was wise
and as wise as he was gentle hearted'. Feeling the in-
justice of Leigh Hunt's imprisonment for having expressed unfavourable opinion of the notorious Prince
Regent, afterwards George IV, he sent his son Cowden each week to the prison in Horsemonger's Lane
with fresh fruit and vegetables. The resulting friendship was passed on in 1816 to Keats. It introduced
him into a circle, whatever may be said of its limitations, that gave immense impetus to his ambition to
become a poet. In advance of his times, Clarke abol-
ished flogging in his school. His scholars were taught
to learn by kindness and by prizes given for volun-
tary work done out of school hours. When Keats left
after eight years of such instruction, he had won
prizes for extra reading and had acquired the gift of
concentration and intensity of thought that is so apparent in his writings.

Of all the friends who counted in the life of John Keats, Cowden Clarke had the greatest influence in shaping his career. When John was brought as a child of seven to Enfield young Clarke, then fifteen years old, gave him much of the elementary part of his education and helped later to form his tastes. Clarke was devoted to music, a lover of the theatre, distinctly literary, and in mature life became a well known critic, lecturer and writer of both prose and occasional poetry. After the younger children in his charge went to bed he often practised on the pianoforte. Both Keats and Edward Holmes, a schoolmate, loved music. Holmes asked their tutor to leave the door open when he played. John remembered it on writing *The Eve of St Agnes* at Bedhampton in the winter of 1819. Reading the poem to Clarke later, he paused at the stanza:

> *The boisterous, midnight, festive clarion,*
> *The kettle-drum, and far-heard clarionet,*
> *Affray his ears, though but in dying tone:*
> *The hall door shuts again, and all the noise is gone.*

and remarked that the last line came into his head because he recollected how he used to listen in bed at school.

Music was in Keats's make up. In the years after he had given up medicine and was still free from the impending tragedy of ailing health and an untimely death, he attended concerts and musical plays as often as slender finances would permit. He sometimes went to recitals at the house of Vincent Novello who lived at 240 Oxford Street in London. Mary Victoria Novello who was then fourteen and later became the wife of Cowden Clarke wrote in her old age:

> *I have even now full recollection of the reverent look with which I regarded John Keats as he leaned against the side of the organ, listening with rapt attention to my father's music. Keats's favourite position – one foot resting on his other knee – still remains imprinted on my memory.*

At the Novello house he heard the best of music: Bach, Haydn, Mozart, Beethoven. Because of his interest in music, Keats told his friend, Benjamin Bailey, whom he visited at Oxford in 1817, that 'had he studied music, he had some notion of the combination of sounds, by which he thought he could have done something as original as his poetry'.

At 19 Lamb's Conduit Street there lived a clever family named Reynolds. Its members included four daughters and one son, John Hamilton Reynolds. After Keats moved to London he became interested in this family. According to Charlotte Reynolds, the youngest daughter, he would listen by the hour to her playing on the pianoforte. There are, among his poems, songs written 'to music as it was playing'.

In the home of Ann and Caroline Mathew, cousins of his friend George Felton Mathew, he also listened to music and composed at least one song:

> *O come dearest Emma!*
> *The rose is full blown.*

Keats was acutely sensitive to harmony. This resulted in smooth rhythms and the soft cadence of his versification. Charlotte Reynolds is authority for his outbursts at a public performance when a wrong note was struck.

Edward Holmes[3] has described Keats at Enfield school:

> *He was a boy whom anyone from his extraordinary vivacity & personal beauty might easily have fancied would become great – but rather in some military capacity than in literature ... In all active exercises – he excelled. The generosity & daring of his character – with the extreme beauty & animation of his face made I remember an impression on me ... this pugnacity and generosity of disposition – in passions of tears or outrageous fits of laughter always in extremes will help to paint Keats in his boyhood. Associated as they were with an extraordinary beauty of person & expression – these qualities captivated the boys, and no one was ever more popular.*

At first, like most healthy, extrovert boys, Keats

preferred playing and exploring to school work. He liked fighting best of all. It took little provocation to bring on a fight. He was nicknamed 'little terrier' and his bravery made him popular. The same intensity showed in him when his affections were stirred or morbid depression set in. Undoubtedly Keats had a vibrant nature. His brother George said that his eyes would moisten and his lips quiver at tales of generosity, distress or noble daring. Popularity among his friends would indicate ready enthusiasm as his usual trait and he was always 'honest minded' and 'honest hearted'.[4] He had, however, fits of melancholy when his thoughts, as was said of Abraham Lincoln, 'would sink into deep caverns where ordinary mortals, whose minds knew not morbidness, would never venture'.

One might expect there would be an abundance of juvenilia by a budding poet. Keats at fifteen began by reading, reading everything, with no revealed inclination toward writing poetry. In the five years that followed, one at school and four as surgeon's apprentice at Edmonton, the strides he made in knowledge were prodigious. By his reading and retentive memory he outfitted himself with a vocabulary which both Tennyson and Swinburne marvelled at. Exclusive of inflected forms it contained more words than Milton used, and almost more than were in the *Odyssey* and *Iliad* combined.[5]

The natural surroundings of the school at Enfield

and the Clarke influence must have given a boy whose
powers of observation and capability of retaining impressions were so extraordinary, a strong leeward
drift towards his hidden unknown career. It is clear
from the burst of interest he took in books, as told by
Cowden Clarke, that he continued all his life to teach
himself. George Meredith used words in his poem
Modern Love that peculiarly, though unintention-
ally, fit the career of Keats:

> *What are we first?*
> *First animals and next*
> *Intelligences at a leap;*
> *On whom,*
> *Pale lies the distant shadow of the tomb*
> *And all that draweth on the tomb for text.*

Keats may well have experienced sudden flowering
in adolescence. His surroundings and the school cur-
riculum took on reality and a 'purpose', a word he
was to cherish later. The evidence is unanimous that
John turned passionately to books. Holmes remembered his reading Macbeth and 'something about
Montezuma & the Incas of Peru'. Clarke said John
devoured all the books in the school library and borrowed more. The school library 'consisted principally
of abridgements of all voyages and travel of any
note: Mavor's *Collection* and *Universal History;*
Robertson's *Histories* of *Scotland, America* and

The parish church of St James at Enfield

The brass of
Lady Tiptoft
*Stated to be the
finest specimen of
such work in England*

Charles V, Miss Edgeworth's novels, Tooke's *Pantheon*, Lemprière's *Classical Dictionary* and Spence's *Polymetis'*. (This last was full of Greek mythology.) The two prizes that Keats won for diligence in reading were Ovid's *Metamorphoses* and Bonnycastle's *Introduction to Astronomy*. It was his memory of the latter and of Robertson's *America* that suggested the famous imagery in the sestet of his sonnet *On First Looking into Chapman's Homer*. Credit for his development must be given also to the daemonic quality of the Keats imagination, to his unique visualisation of objects observed in nature and memory of words read, above all to his skill in using the tightest word that would fit concretely what he had to say.

An interesting incidence of boyish impressions, recalled later, appears to have resulted from his attending church at Enfield School. It can be admitted that Keats was never much given to religious rites but his repeated visits at church and keen observation had their effect. The Enfield parish church dedicated to St Andrew, dating in part from the twelfth century, was not then modernised. It was an old country parish church in a countryside. In it was, and still is, a medieval monument to Lady Tiptoft, a lady of royal descent, whose effigy in brass has, besides its emblems of greatness, an unusual half-mantle covering. Jacosa Lady Tiptoft, mother of the famous Earl of Worcester beheaded on Tower Hill in 1470, lived

C

in Worcester Manor House and was buried at Enfield.

When I visited the parish church in 1951 and saw this very fine brass of the fifteenth century, it occurred to me that the figure placed in the floor of the church must have given Keats his early idea of the trappings of chivalry. Lady Tiptoft is represented with the quaint horned headgear of the period, surmounted by a coronet, in an elaborately embroidered and jewelled costume consisting of a sleeveless jacket and a long gown enriched with ermine, partly concealed by a mantle embroidered with the arms of her father and those of her mother. The alert eyes of Keats, a devotee of chivalry, must have taken in these details and sparkled over them.

As a medical student in 1815-16, beginning to lean heavily towards poetry, Keats was intimate for a time with George Felton Mathew. In the Mathew group was a girl named Mary Frogley, a centre of interest to all young men. Upon his moving to London, John and his brother George, fired with the spirit of romance, seem to have been associated in a partnership to which John supplied sentimental valentines for amorous purposes. John's poem beginning 'Hadst Thou lived when chivalry' (published much altered from the valentine in his 1817 volume) was written for George to send to Mary Frogley. John remembered Lady Tiptoft's effigy. It supplied some of the details of the excessively romantic appeal of George

to Mary. The following stanza copied from the valentine is recorded in Richard Woodhouse's scrapbook
(now in the Pierpont Morgan Library in New York):

> *Hadst thou liv'd when chivalry*
> *Lifted up her lance on high,*
> *Tell me what thou wouldst have been.*
> *Ah! I see the silver sheen*
> *Of thy broidered, floating vest*
> *Cov'ring half thine ivory breast;*
> *Which, O heavens! I should see,*
> *But that cruel destiny*
> *Has placed a golden cuirass there;*
> *Keeping secret what is fair.*
> *Like light in wreathed cloudlets nested*
> *Thy hair in gilden casque is rested.*

To vivacious Mary Frogley we are indebted for the
preservation of many of Keats's early verses. Mary,
who became the wife of Dr William Henry Neville of
Usher, is said to have had a keen interest in the poet's
career.

Also in Enfield there was at that time the epitaph
of Anne Gery, a young girl who died in 1643. The
chancel floor held a brass plate with the Gery arms
and this inscription:

> *Here lies enterr'd*
> *One that scarce err'd*
> *A virgin modest, free from folly*
> *A virgin knowing patient, holy*

A virgin blest with beauty here
A virgin crowned with glory there
To the precious memory of Anne Gery daughter of
Richard Gery Esquire of Bushmead.[6]

The form of this unique verse must have been registered in John's photographic memory. In adopting a
new form of prosody first disclosed in his journal letter of December 1818 to George he appears to have
remembered it. He wrote two poems in that letter
with this explanation: 'These are specimens of a sort
of rondeau which I think I shall become partial to —
because you have one idea amplified with greater
ease and more delight and freedom than in the sonnet'.

The idea of a virgin blest on earth and also crowned
in heaven probably suggested to Keats the double
immortality of poets which he made the subject of
his so called rondeau. Tom had died on 1st December
1818, after much suffering. Love for his dying brother and appreciation of Tom's sweet and faultless
nature very likely brought to mind the little girl of
Enfield church. The purity of Tom's life on earth like
the girl's of Enfield church and the glory awaiting
them in Heaven may, also, have inspired John with
the thought of transmuting the idea of double immortality (suggested by the epitaph) to the broader
basis of the poem which he sent George shortly after
Tom's death.

> *Bards of Passion and of Mirth*
> *Ye have left your souls on earth!*
> *Have ye souls in heaven too,*
> *Double-lived in regions new?*

The entire rondeau of which only the first stanza is quoted represents a single idea as the Enfield epitaph did.

The death of his father in 1804 had little apparent effect on John or his brothers and sister because of their youth; but his mother's death from tuberculosis in March 1810 left John heartbroken. He is said to have tenderly cared for her during vacations, even cooking her meals. His school friend, Edward Holmes, wrote to R. M. Milnes, first of the poet's biographers, that Keats, learning at school of her death gave way to prolonged and impassioned grief. He hid, inconsolable under the master's desk. Fate, never kind in his lifetime, soon delivered another blow in the appointment of Richard Abbey as guardian of the Keats minor children and trustee of their property. John was to find dealing with him difficult, sometimes impossible, especially in his strict control over Fanny Keats.

Mrs John Jennings (aged seventy-four), after her daughter's death, realising that the Keats children had no near living relative except herself, turned to two old friends for help. She made Richard Abbey, a

prosperous tea broker, and John Rowland Sandell
trustees of most of the property her husband had left,
retiring herself from any business control of it. When
she died in December 1814 the last link snapped in
the chain that tied the Keats children to their past.
Abbey and Sandell took custody of Fanny Keats then
aged eleven. The two younger boys, George and Tom,
were already employed in Abbey's tea business. Abbey was always friendly with George and later fav-
oured him. Also he attempted to make a hatter out of
'poor Tom' by sending him to Lyons, but soon lost
interest in the sickly youth. He never, however, un-
derstood and could barely tolerate the independent
spirit of his oldest ward, who spurned all efforts to
make him into a hatter or a tea broker or even an
apothecary. Sandell as co-trustee soon gave up and
went away, leaving Abbey in sole control of the minor
children and their property.

Abbey dealt in tea at 4 Pancras Lane, in the Poultry, London, and had in addition an interest in a hat
making concern. He lived with a wife and adopted
daughter over his shop in winter, in summer at Walthamstow. During her minority he kept Fanny Keats
practically a prisoner. Fanny recovered her share of
the Keats family property after some delay in 1824
on coming of age.

In 1811, the year Abbey became guardian, John
was turning into a man. Perhaps Abbey advised his

grandmother that he was unfitted for trade and, being bookish, should be trained for the profession of medicine. That can be done, he could have told her, in Edmonton right near her own house. It is easy to understand how the prospect of being near his grandmother, whom he adored, and also only two miles away from his admired friend and wise mentor Cowden Clarke would please Keats. He had come to realise that he had a mind capable of grasping any mental problem. The apothecary job, if one had to earn a living, was as good as anything. After all he had his books and his dreams.

He complacently acquiesced in being apprenticed for five years to Thomas Hammond, the Edmonton surgeon. He could continue his self imposed task of translating into prose all twelve books of Virgil's *Aeneid*. Probably once a week or so he could get off, walk over to Enfield to see Tom who was still at school, exchange books and discuss his reading with his old tutor. Since Abbey had paid Hammond an unusually high fee – 200 guineas – instead of the usual apprentice fee of £40, John must have been something of a star boarder.

A fellow apprentice is said to have described Keats as 'a loafing fellow always quoting poetry'. This may have been jealousy of the ordinary apprentice who paid only £40 and was assigned to menial tasks. Keats was quick and able. We know that in his early months at Guy's Hospital he was appointed a 'dresser' so it is difficult to believe him a shirker at Hammond's. He lived in a room over the surgery known afterwards as 'Keats's Cottage', and usually attended Hammond on his calls. Certainly he was free to pursue his own thoughts in his spare time. He was maturing fast mentally and probably felt himself so grown up that he chuckled over the time he lived at the Clarke school successfully disguised to himself as a child. He had come a long way and was both proud and confident.

Going back to Enfield school was second nature to him. The remains of the ancient Middlesex forest bordering the path he took from Edmonton contained some fine oak trees. They became 'Those green-rob'd senators of mighty woods, Tall oaks branch-charmed by the earnest stars' when he wrote *Hyperion*. Clarke thought all their meetings took place whenever possible in the old arbour of the school garden. We should like to have been able to listen to their discussions. Clarke was well acquainted with Shakespeare, Milton and Spenser and with many other Elizabethan and Jacobean writers. He thought less of Pope and the eighteenth century poets. It was the revival of renaissance poetry in that century, neverthless, that stirred their talks.

Keats was an apt pupil with his mental powers becoming highly developed. He read constantly but it had not yet occurred to him to try to express his thoughts in writing. It was only after three years of growth and study that his pen found itself. These two enthusiastic youths, chatting together in the arbour during the long twilight, discussed books and the politics of those exciting days that witnessed Napoleon's rise and fall. They discussed also Leigh Hunt, still in prison, and the liberal ideas of *The Examiner* of which Hunt was publisher. Clarke lent *The Examiner* to Keats and wrote later that it no doubt laid the foundation of his love of civil and religious liberty.

It was a banner day when Clarke introduced Spenser to Keats who took back with him to Edmonton that same night the volume of *The Faerie Queene* through which he 'ramped like a young horse turned into a Spring meadow'. Reading Spenser opened up a new, enchantingly romantic world. Here were the familiar knights and ladies of boyhood's fancy transmuted into real adventurers who dwelt in 'strange and monstrous' woods. They gave a reality to the airy creatures of his imagination that they never lost. Reading Spenser probably released whatever inhibition he was experiencing about expressing himself.

Keats was always glad to be with his old tutor whose buoyant nature and never gloomy disposition stimulated him. There was time enough too at Enfield for the music making that he loved. But until

almost the end of his apprenticeship John did not let
his brothers know of trying his hand at copying Spenser's style of poetry. He was also reticent and even
shy concerning the first poem he showed Clarke, who
never knew Keats wrote poetry until he saw on the
day of Hunt's release from prison, 3rd February 1815,
John's fanciful tribute to him. Without confiding in
his brothers or Clarke he had secretly written at Edmonton his *Imitation of Spenser* (perhaps his first
attempt at verse), a sonnet *On Peace* and in the summer of 1814 a sensuous poem celebrating the beauties
of an unknown lady seen at Vauxhall, beginning 'Fill
for me a brimming bowl'. He wrote a sonnet to Lord
Byron in December 1814, another *To Chatterton*
probably in January 1815. He produced in February
an *Ode to Apollo*, the apostrophe *To Hope* in the
same month and in May an epigram 'Infatuate Bri-
tons', reviling the tyranny of Charles II.

Clarke had moved to Clerkenwell and Keats was
seeing the Mathew family in his spare time. He sent
some verses to the Misses Mathew on vacation at
Hastings in 1815 and received from them in return a
curious shell and a copy of verses by Tom Moore.
This inspired him with further sentimentality which
ended in a self satisfied salute to their cousin, George
Felton Mathew, who was also at Hastings. The eighteenth century revival of renaissance poetry set the
style or genre of his poems written at Edmonton. He

imitated all sorts of writers, using different versifica-
tions and words that he chose from memory of his
various readings from Shakespeare, Milton, Spenser,
Mary Tighe, Charlotte Smith, Wieland's *Oberon,*
Thomson, Young, Cooper, Gray, Collins, Leigh Hunt,
and Lord Byron. He was distinctly an imitator.

In 1814 the ties which until now had bound him
happily to Edmonton were severed. When his grandmother died in December, life became different for
John Keats. Whether or not he turned to his guardian
we do not know; at any rate Abbey decided to take a
hand. He said something must be done to advance
the career of medicine. His ward had learned all he
could or would from Hammond. The time had come
to break the bond of servitude. With his fee in hand
for five full years of apprenticeship, Hammond was
content to reduce them to four. So in his twentieth
year, bearing with him the necessary certificate of
good behaviour from Hammond, John entered Guy's
Hospital at the 'Borough' in London, on 1st October
1815, to begin a new and fateful career. He carried
with him too, the gift of making friends and holding
their loyalty – 'a peculiar sweetness of expression'
when in their company.

The training given him at the Clarke school, his
character and determination, his attractive personality, his mental growth during his apprenticeship
and the 'basic material' his brain had absorbed in

Middlesex, combined to produce the special equipment he needed to meet the demands of his genius.

CHAPTER TWO

GUY'S HOSPITAL AND THE END OF
MEDICINE: 1815-16

PROBABLY with a great deal of enthusiasm Keats moved to London. By crossing nearby London Bridge, he could go to his brothers at Abbey's in 4 Pancras Lane or to see his friend Mathew with whom he liked to exchange fanciful song and strange tales of elf and fay. Life must have seemed freer and more independent than at Hammond's. In 'O Solitude', the first poem he wrote in London shortly after his arrival, he contrasted his lot 'among the jumbled heap of murky buildings' with the 'flowery slopes' of the countryside he had left behind in Middlesex. He may have lived at 8 Dean Street, off Tooley Street, about three hundred yards from the hospital, the address he gave Cowden Clarke in September 1816, after his return from Margate, before going to join his brothers in the Poultry. Later in 1815, however, he shared rooms with other medical students, at a tallow chandler's named Markham, in St Thomas's Street near Guy's.

The brief hospital career of Keats may seem to lovers of his poetry to have little to do with the poems he wrote; yet it was important as experience gained from contact with humanity in the mass and in further intense training of his already acute powers of

observation. It enlarged his viewpoint in a field he
would not have known had he 'stayed upon the green
shore and piped a silly pipe', a phrase he was to use
later to justify his struggle over *Endymion*. Many of
his friends profited by his medical counsel. No doubt
'ailing' James Rice did and John Reynolds. When the
latter complained of tedious recovery from serious
illness, Keats assured him:

> *All Medical Men will tell you how far a very gradual*
> *amendment is preferable; you will be strong after*
> *this, never fear.*

To little Mrs Dilke, a close friend of all the Keats brothers and a sufferer from gallstones, he apparently
gave friendly advice from time to time. He told his
brother George:

> *I dare say you have altered also – every man does –*
> *our bodies every seven years are completely fresh*
> *materiald*[7] ...

His knowledge of pharmacy sometimes supplied apt
jokes. He wrote Benjamin Bailey in March 1818 from
Teignmouth describing Devon men, whom he thought
a feminine lot, as 'Pulvis Ipecac Simplex – a strong
dose' (in other words, nauseating).
  John used medical similes as figures of comparison
in *Endymion* and both 'Hyperions', the *Ode to Fanny,*

Isabella, Cap and Bells and *Otho the Great,* especially those pertaining to blood or bleeding of which he
was fated later to be a victim. In 'I stood tip-toe',
while still walking the hospital in the autumn of 1816,
remembering the fevered patients in its wards, he
wrote at Hampstead a physician's ideal prescription
for such sufferers:

> *The breezes were ethereal, and pure,*
> *And crept through half closed lattices to cure*
> *The languid sick; it cool'd their fever'd sleep,*
> *And soothed them into slumbers full and deep.*
> *Soon they awoke clear eyed: nor burnt with*
>   *thirsting,*
> *Nor with hot fingers, nor with temples bursting:*

In assessing his later work in poetry it is not wise to
consider the four years at Edmonton and his year and
a half attached to Guy's Hospital as wasted effort.
He had not entirely matured in 1816. Time and experience were needed to reach the heights of 1819.

Having come from the country to live in London,
Keats must have been impressed by the fact that he
was treading in the footsteps of the great Elizabethans. London at both ends of old London Bridge had
been alive with the activities of the early dramatists
and actors. In the neighbourhood of St Saviour's
Church, opposite Guy's Hospital, there once existed
a section known as 'liberty of the clink' where the

Globe and also the Rose Theatre, both built for Shakespeare, were located.[8]

Apothecaries Hall, where Keats registered for the
hospital, was at Blackfriars close by the site of a play-
house Shakespeare had both owned and acted in. If
the poetically minded medical student walked down
Bread Street to the Thames from Cheapside, he would
pass the sites of the Mermaid Tavern and John Milton's birthplace. Fresh from saturation with Edmund
Spenser and Michael Drayton at Edmonton he could
now add further to his Elizabethan education.

Though a revival of the master's plays was taking
place during the Regency of the Prince Consort with
Edmund Kean performing, whose acting, Coleridge
said, was like 'reading Shakespeare by flashes of lightning,' there are no extant letters to tell us what Keats
was thinking in 1815. Besides the Mathew group and
his own brothers, the only persons known to be in
touch with him, other than medical students, were
William Haslam, Joseph Severn, Edward Holmes and
Charles J. Wells (a friend and classmate of Tom's).
Of the medical students the one he was most interested in seems to have been Henry Stephens, who liked
poetry and turned up several times later in John's life.
Another fellow student, Walter Cooper Dendy, who
published in 1841 *The Philosophy of Mystery*, told
in it how John filled the time of an anatomy lesson by
writing in medieval form, a version of an old French

lay (*Lai d'Aristote*) about Alexander's meeting an Indian maid of surpassing beauty on his march through
India.

   At Guy's Hospital John enrolled in seven courses,
two on anatomy and physiology, two on the theory
and practice of medicine, two on chemistry and one
on *Materia Medica*. All this meant more onerous
duties than at Edmonton. As for his rhyming he was
too level headed to think of himself yet as a poet.
Fancy was in his make up, however, and he could not
help living it. The novelty and excitement of hospital
work aroused his interest for the time being and absorbed him conscientiously. He was the first dresser
appointed from his class. That gave him some pres-
tige. The surgeon he was assigned to, William Lucas
Junior, was an ungainly man and a sloppy operator
but John, as a student, had the privilege of sitting
under Astley Cooper, a surgeon of real ability, who
was said, by achieving knighthood, to have 'raised
surgery from a trade to a profession'. Keats's note-
book on anatomy and physiology, which is at Hampstead, shows he was well taught. It is full of what 'C'
said and proves John a serious student of medicine.
He was more interested in physiology, and the treatment of disease in general, than in bone structure. He
sometimes drew flowers in the margin of the note-
book while listening to anatomy lectures. His sense
of humour is evident in one remark he wrote down:

D

*In disease Medical Men guess, if they cannot ascer-
tain a disease they call it nerveous.*

Besides indicating John's interest in the courses Astley Cooper taught, the letter 'C' quoted in his note-
book may have applied also to James Curry who
lectured on *materia medica* and practice.

A student named John Flint South,[9] who preceded
Keats by two years, has told the story of conditions
which prevailed at Guy's during that period. The
worst feature of hospital practice in 1815 was the
reliance of demonstrators in anatomy on 'body
snatchers' who robbed graves to provide bodies for
dissection. Corpses usually brought four guineas
apiece. The demonstrator of dissection was Joseph
Henry Green whom John was to meet again on the
occasion of his interview with Coleridge at Millfield
Lane, Highgate in May 1819. Only less revolting than
body snatching was the surgery itself. Before the use
of antiseptics and ether, operations at best were
dirty, weird and horrible. Keats as dresser carried a
'tin plaister box', a sort of badge of office. The dressers, and students in general, crowded round the
operating table, often in such a mob that the surgeon
could with difficulty perform an operation. The atmosphere was stifling and the unfortunate patients
had to suffer without anaesthetics.

Dressers were the forerunners of house surgeons

in modern hospitals. They took turns, week by week, in charge of the wards, served out-patients, pulled teeth, performed blood letting, decided what cases required surgical treatment and attended lectures in their chosen courses. When the surgeon arrived at the hospital, the dresser who served him had to be on hand to accompany him from bed to bed. The surgeon would usually first treat the wound, leaving his assistant to change the dressings which, before advent of antiseptic surgery, often festered quickly. Mr Lucas, though pleasant and likeable, was not a skillful surgeon and students apparently did not crowd around or follow him as he shuffled through the wards.

With Astley Cooper, who was handsome, tall and already famous, it was different. Students had to fight for a place to hear and watch the great man. It was a tribute both to personality and, no doubt, to John's excellence as a medical student that caused Astley Cooper to pick out 'little Keats' for special attention. On his recommendation to his own dresser and relative, George Cooper, John was able to move from his solitary, murky lodging to room with Cooper, Frederick Tyrell, George Wilson Mackereth and Henry Stephens in St Thomas's Street nearby the hospital. When Cooper and Tyrell left the hospital in 1816, he joined Stephens and Mackereth alone.

Thirty years later Stephens[10] wrote to George

Felton Mathew his impression of his room mate.

> *Whether it was in the latter part of the year 1815 or the early part of the year 1816 that my acquaintance with John Keats commenced I cannot say. We were both students at the United Hospitals of St Thomas' and Guy's, and we had apartments in the house in St Thomas' Street kept by a decent respectable woman by the name of Mitchell, I think . . . John Keats, being alone, and to avoid the expense of having a Sitting Room to himself, asked to join us, which we readily acceded to. We were therefore constant companions . . . He had been apprenticed to a Mr Hammond, surgeon of Southgate, from whence he came on the completion of his time to the Hospitals. His passion if I may so call it for poetry was soon manifested . . . He attended lectures and went through the usual routine, but he had no desire to excel in that pursuit.*
>
> *Poetry was to his mind the zenith of all his Aspirations — The only thing worthy the attention of superior minds — So he thought — All other pursuits were mean and tame. He had no idea of Fame or Greatness but as it was connected with the pursuits of Poetry, or the Attainment of Poetical excellence — the greatest men in the world were the Poets, and to rank among them was the chief object of his ambition . . . He had two Brothers, who visited him frequently, and they worshipped him. They seemed to think their Brother John was to be exalted and to exalt the family name . . . He was gentlemanly in his manners*

and when he condescended to talk upon other sub-
jects he was agreeable and intelligent. He was quick
and apt at learning, when he chose to give his atten-
tion to any subject. He was a steady quiet and well
behaved person, never inclined to pursuits of a low
or vicious Character.

I remember the time of his first introduction to Mr
Leigh Hunt, who then edited The Examiner, *and I*
remember several pieces of his poetry being inserted
in that Journal, at which he was exceedingly grati-
fied. I remember his also telling me of an introduc-
tion he had to three Young Poets of Promise and
among them I remember well the name of Shelley.

Even if Stephens may have thought Keats indifferent
towards his hospital duties, his ability is shown by the
fact that Mackereth and he went up for examination
at the same time, 25th July 1816. Keats passed and
Mackereth did not.

When the tour of duty at the hospital had ended
for the day John would turn his thoughts to poetry.
His attitude of quiet rebellion was reflected in his
poem addressed in November 1815 to the 'Kindred
Spirit' of his poetical friend, Mathew. He had for
some time been reading Shakespeare, Spenser, Milton and Wordsworth and eighteenth century verse of
the most fanciful and romantic nature with Mathew.
They copied each other's airy ideas and even used the
same words. Until Keats grew beyond the poetical

range of Mathew and Leigh Hunt in 1818 and climbed skyward taking Shakespeare and Milton for guides he wrote only occasional, first rate verse. The poetry he imitated was lush and artificial.

Jane Austen, a keen and humorous observer, had published in 1811 her novel, *Sense and Sensibility*. She looked out of the windows of her Chawton cottage at a world infected with sensibility, meaning exceptional openness to emotional impressions. In her novel she made a contrast between sense, sagacity and control in her heroine, Elinor Dashwood, and an over supply of sensibility in Marianne, Elinor's sister, who was 'everything but prudent'. If John had come across Jane Austen's novel in 1816, his alert sense of humour might have kept him from the excess of sentimentality which later made him the target for bitter attacks by Scottish reviewers. As it was he couldn't resist Mathew's silly reply, addressed 'To a poetical friend,' containing fulsome praise of a fanciful Keats. It was perhaps natural that a romantic medical student should seek relief from grim hospital duties in fanciful dreams but his tongue must have been in his cheek when he himself described the melancholy Mathew as changing from a blooming 'flowret' to a fish of gold and ending up as a black eyed swan.

During 1816, however, Keats came in touch again with William Haslam and, through him, with Joseph Severn. These two were to devote themselves to the

poet's interests until the end. As a result, his sentimental connection with Mathew appears to have
faded into the limbo of forgotten things. Haslam
turned out to be the most reliable friend Keats had.
Though little is known of his early life, he was probably born in the same year as the poet, grew up to
be a solicitor and succeeded on his father's death to
the position held by the latter in Frampton and Sons,
Wholesale Grocers. Charles Brown said Haslam and
John were schoolfellows. That seems doubtful since
Cowden Clarke, their schoolmaster, apparently never
was in touch with Haslam. But Severn, as if to con-
firm a long standing friendship, wrote to R. M. Milnes
after the poet's death that Haslam was 'intimate with
Keats on his leaving school'. He was one of the earliest
of the poet's friends.

A practical non-literary man, Haslam did not figure
much in Keats's correspondence. He exchanged many
letters with Severn and followed closely the vicissi-
tudes of the poet. He kept in touch with Tom when
John was in Scotland and acted as mailing agent in
the dispatch of John's letters to George in America.
After his tour of Scotland with Charles Brown in
1818, John wrote George: 'I cannot forbear mentioning Haslam as a most kind and obliging and constant
friend – his behaviour to Tom during my absence
and since my return has endeared him to me for ever.'
On 4th December 1820, Haslam wrote to Severn at

Rome: 'Keats must get himself well again, Severn, if
but for us. I, for one, cannot afford to lose him. If I
know what it is to love, I truly love John Keats'.

There can be no doubt that Haslam was, as Severn
justly described him, an 'Oak friend'. His friendship
was the kind that time cannot wilt. In 1845 he wrote to
R. M. Milnes: 'Poor Keats – thirty years ago the world
thought not for itself as now it does. Party was everything. Keats, as has been said of others, stood on the
shoulders of the age – what Keats, young as he was,
felt and feeling could not but give forth – what the
Sycophants of that day crushed him for giving utter-
ance to, has since become accepted truth to tens of
thousands'.

Severn, two years older than Keats, was a struggling painter. Their bond at first was a 'mutual love of
nature'. The poet's superior mind opened up a new
world to Severn. They made excursions into the fields,
John acting as guide and philosopher. On the walks
in the country, nothing escaped him, Severn said –
the song of a bird, the rustle of some animal, the lights
and shadows, the wayfaring of the clouds, the colour
of a woman's hair, the smile of a child or the features
of passing tramps! This period of their friendship
was described later by Severn in a letter to Charles
Brown:

I was introduced to him by Haslam. He was then

studying at Guy's Hospital, yet much inclined to the Muses. I remember on the second meeting he read me a sonnet on Solitude. He was at that time more playful in his manner: the world seem'd to have nothing to do with him. Poetry was evidently at that time his darling hope.

He disliked surgery and complained that his guardian, Mr Abbey, forced him to it against his will. He was introduced to Mr Hunt which wrought a great change in him. It confirmed him in his future career and I think intoxicated him with an excess of enthusiasm.

Keats said of Severn that he was the 'most astonishingly suggestive innocent' he had ever met. But Severn's love of art, of music and his general appreciation of the beautiful had no little influence on the poet who always learned from his friends. The experience of others was never lost on him. Especially he enjoyed the visits with Severn to art museums.

While sticking resolutely to his medical course in the winter of 1815-16, Keats dreamed all the time, doubtless, about the chivalric and pastoral poetry of Spenser as adapted by seventeenth century writers. Leigh Hunt published in February 1816 *The Story of Rimini,* a romance of chivalry. John eagerly read it. He was yet to meet Hunt but he admired his natural style of writing and at once began to imitate it. He soon wrote *Specimen of an Induction to a Poem,* and

Calidore: A Fragment (with Cockney frills of chivalry); also a sonnet to an unknown sweetheart of his whom he described as 'sweeter by far than Hybla's honied roses'. It was soon to be the summer of 1816 — the time Keats must take his examination for the right to practise surgery. Yet even before he went up for his examination he wrote a bevy of sonnets. One of them was written in the fields in June, beginning 'To one who has been long in city pent'. Another expressed his longing for the country where he could muse 'on a fair summer's eve' about 'Milton's Fate' and drop a tear to sorrow induced by 'poesy'.

With examinations over and his degree in his pocket John made straight for Margate on the seashore at the end of July 1816, taking Tom with him – the first time, I believe, he had ever left London or the familiar scenes of his boyhood. He was still under age. His guardian, Abbey, had arranged his career for him. He was supposed to practise his profession at Tottenham in nearby and familiar Middlesex. Before deciding against a professional career in medicine he did some soul searching at Margate and waited until his twenty-first birthday had come and gone before confronting Abbey with his decision. In the epistle sent from Margate to George he expressed doubt of the wisdom of abandoning medicine but made clear his rebellion against it in favour of greater happiness to himself in poetry:

Full many a dreary hour have I past,
My brain bewildered and my mind o'ercast
With Heaviness; in seasons, when I've thought
No spherey strains, by me, could e'er be caught
From the blue Dome, though I to dimness Gaze
On the far depth, where sheeted Lightning plays;
Or, on the wavy Grass outstretch'd supinely,
Pry 'mong the Stars, to strive to think divinely:
That I should never hear Appollo's song . . .
. . . Ah, my dear friend and brother!
Could I, at once, my real Ambition smother
For tasting Joys like these; sure I should be
Happier, and dearer to society . . .

In the same mood he explained in September his waverings to his tutor, Cowden Clarke, and acknowledged his great indebtedness to him:

With shatter'd boat, oar snapt, and canvas rent,
I slowly sail, scarce knowing my intent;
Still scooping up the waters with my fingers,
In which a trembling diamond never lingers.
By this, friend Charles, you may full plainly see
Why I have never penn'd a line to thee:
Because my thoughts were never free, and clear
And little fit to please a classic ear . . .
Nor should I now, but that I've known you long;
That you first taught me all the sweets of song;
The grand, the sweet, the terse, the free, the fine,
What swell'd with pathos, and what right divine:
Spenserian vowels that elope with ease
And float along like birds o'er summer seas . . .

Who let me taste that more than cordial dram,
The sharp, the rapier-pointed epigram?
Shew'd me that epic was of all the king
Round vast and spanning all like Saturn's ring?
    Ah! had I never seen,
Or known your kindness, what might I have
    been?
What my enjoyments in my youthful years,
Bereft of all that now my life endears?
And can I e'er these benefits forget?
And can I e'er repay the friendly debt?
No, doubly no;

His vacation over John returned to London and duti-
fully went back to his job at the hospital. There is a
suggestion in the letter written on 9th October 1816,
inviting Cowden Clarke to 8 Dean Street in the Borough, that he may have gone back to live in his old
lodging near the hospital. If so, he soon afterwards
joined his brothers in the Poultry across the river.

The exact date when Keats turned his back finally
on the career of medicine and slammed the door in
the face of Abbey is uncertain. Since Stephens remembered seeing him (probably at the hospital) after
he had become associated with Leigh Hunt and Shelley, his break with medicine may not have occurred
until the beginning of 1817. Whenever it happened,
the meeting between him and Abbey was bound to
be momentous and historic. Abbey's account of the

encounter was given in 1827 to John Taylor, Keats's
publisher, who, at that time planned to write a life of
the poet:

*It was Mr Abbey's advice, that John should com-
mence Business at Tottenham as a Surgeon. He communicated his Plans to his Ward, but his Surprise
was not moderate, to hear in Reply, that he did not
intend to be a Surgeon — Not intend to be a Surgeon!
Why what do you mean to be? I mean to rely on my
Abilities as a Poet — John you are either Mad or a
Fool, to talk in so absurd a Manner. My mind is
made up, said the youngster very quietly. I know
that I possess Abilities greater than most Men, and
therefore I am determined to gain my Living by
exercising them – Seeing nothing could be done Abbey called him a Silly Boy, & prophesied a speedy
Termination to his inconsiderate Enterprise.*

Shortly after John's return to London, he wrote to
Clarke, whom he had not seen while at the hospital,
from his Dean Street address, as already mentioned.
That gesture from his old friend, according to Clarke,
preceded their 'first symposium' which took place at
Clerkenwell late in October 1816. A Mr Alsager had
lent Chapman's translation to Clarke in the folio edition of 1616. Together they pored over it until day-
break. Keats walked home to Dean Street in the dawn
and on the way a great poem was born. His mind
went back to his school days and the thrill he felt on

reading Robertson's *History of America*. In his exhilaration he was the explorer. 'Then felt I like' and he wrote what he himself saw. His sensation was that of Balboa, whom he called Cortez, standing among his men and coming suddenly, for the first time in man's history, on a vast and unexplored ocean. His imagination was not to reach such heights again until after his return from the broadening experience of the Scottish tour and he had fallen in love with Fanny Brawne.

In the published version of the sonnet John Keats changed only two lines of the original octave and altered the famous sestet not at all:

> Much have I travell'd in the realms of gold,
> And many goodly states and kingdoms seen;
> Round many western islands have I been
> Which bards in fealty to Apollo hold.
> Oft of one wide expanse had I been told
> That deep-brow'd Homer ruled as his demesne;
> Yet did I never breathe its pure serene
> Till I heard Chapman speak out loud and bold:
> Then felt I like some watcher of the skies
> When a new planet swims into his ken;
> Or like stout Cortez when with eagle eyes
> He star'd at the Pacific – and all his men
> Look'd at each other with a wild surmise –
> Silent, upon a peak in Darien.

Cowden Clarke has explained the astonishing speed

at which it was composed: 'When I came down to
breakfast the next morning, I found upon my table a
letter with no other enclosure than this famous sonnet . . . We had parted, as I have already said, at dayspring yet he contrived that I should receive the poem
from a distance of, maybe two miles, by ten o'clock'.
With 'teeming wonderment' Clarke decided to sub-
mit to his friend Hunt the 'Chapman's Homer' sonnet
and a few earlier poems written by Keats.

CHAPTER THREE

POETRY TAKES COMMAND AT HAMPSTEAD: 1817

WHEN KEATS was taken to Hunt's cottage in the Vale of Health at Hampstead it was, as Clarke said, 'a red letter day in the young poet's life'. He became a familiar of the household, 'always welcomed'. Inclusion in the Hunt circle had important results. It brought him, an embryo poet, into a brilliant circle of poets, musicians, painters and critics. There began his friendship with John Hamilton Reynolds to whom he revealed his poetical theories more intimately than to anyone else except to George in America. He also met Shelley, Haydon, Horace Smith, Vincent Novello, William Godwin, Charles Lamb, William Hazlitt and Basil Montagu. In the beginning, perhaps, John was ill at ease. When Horace Smith, a social lion, called at Hunt's cottage he found the young poet alone and remembered that 'his manner was shy and embarrassed as of one unused to society and he spoke little', but he soon found himself.

Leigh Hunt who sponsored Keats was well known in the literary world and a popular martyr to the principles of liberty. John in his epistle written to Clarke from Margate spoke with open envy of the 'sweet forest walks' the latter had taken with 'wrong'd Libertas',

E

as he, in knightly fashion, dubbed Hunt. An amusing talker and acute critic, Hunt loved and attracted a following. Keats admired him greatly. They discussed poetry, walked in the fields about Hampstead and matched each other's skill in writing impromptu verses. They used to play a sort of game competing against time in the composition of poetry. Clarke was present at one such occasion on 30th December 1816, when Keats won, as to time and quality, with his sonnet *On the Grasshopper and Cricket* in what has been called a 'miracle of improvisation'. No wonder John felt elated. He was young, attractive, confident and was living among men of reputation and achievement whom he meant to equal.

One December night, on walking home to 76 Cheapside where the brothers were then lodging, he expressed his happy thoughts:

> Keen, fitful gusts are whisp'ring here and there
> Among the bushes half leafless, and dry;
> The stars look very cold about the sky,
> And I have many miles on foot to fare.
> Yet feel I little of the cool bleak air,
> Or of the dead leaves rustling drearily,
> Or of those silver lamps that burn on high,
> Or of the distance from home's pleasant lair:
> For I am brimful of the friendliness
> That in a little cottage I have found;
> Of fair-hair'd Milton's eloquent distress,

And all his love for gentle Lycid drown'd;
Of lovely Laura in her light green dress,
And faithful Petrarch gloriously crown'd.

The new life John was experiencing teemed with excitement and surprises. On 1st December 1816, Hunt published in *The Examiner* an unsigned article entitled 'Young Poets'. It stated that the object of the article was 'merely to mention three young writers' (Shelley, Keats and Reynolds) and went on to give a friendly criticism of Keats. On the same day Hunt composed a sonnet ending: 'I see, ev'n now, young Keats a flowering laurel on your brow'. Much excited, John conceived in December the idea of writing a long poem *(Endymion)*; he also composed as his tribute to nature, 'I stood tip-toe upon a little hill', and outlined the plan of his career in *Sleep and Poetry*, in which he promised himself to luxuriate in the realm of Flora and old Pan, to 'choose each pleasure that my fancy sees' and finally to abandon them

> *for a nobler life*
> *Where I may find the agonies, the strife,*
> *Of human hearts.*

Sleep and Poetry (in which he described the effect on him of his surroundings) was thought out during a night spent on the couch in the sitting room of Hunt's cottage.

294437

LIBRARY
FLORIDA STATE UNIVERSITY
TALLAHASSEE, FLORIDA

Cowden Clarke has described the pleasant activities of the Hunt circle at this period:

> *The evenings of chamber music at Vincent Novello's, where Leigh Hunt, Shelley, Keats, and the Lambs were invited guests; the brilliant supper parties at the alternate dwellings of the Novellos, the Hunts, and the Lambs, who had mutually agreed that bread and cheese, with celery and Elia's immortalized 'Lutheran beer' were to be the sole eates provided; . . . and the picnic repasts enjoyed together by an appointment in the fields that then lay spread in green breadth and luxuriance between the west end of Oxford Street and the western slope of Hampstead Hill . . . are things never to be forgotten.*

We do not know how many of these jolly, simple festivities Keats attended but they are a sample of the happy opportunities of his new experiences.

Keats was not alone in admiring Hunt whom Hazlitt, Lamb, Moore, Rogers and Byron, all praised. But he had a purpose deeper than anything Hunt was capable of. Before the winter wore away he was aware of certain vulgar limitations in his new friend and ceased to regard him as the model he had first thought. During the winter, however, his wagon stayed definitely hitched to the star of Hunt. Publishing his first volume of poems at his mentor's suggestion, he prefaced it with a flattering dedicatory

sonnet. Hunt, feeling he was sponsoring Keats, expressed disapproval of the proposed plan of composition of *Endymion,* much to the annoyance of his young
friend who thought he, as poet, was being dictated to.
Their friendship, after its short winter honeymoon,
became rather one sided so far as poetical confiden-
ces were concerned. John gave George his opinion of
Hunt as a good-natured, vain and coarse egoist, who
'does one harm by making fine things petty and beautiful things hateful', an appraisal accurate at the time,
no doubt, yet a phase the genial Hunt outgrew in his
maturity. 'He is,' wrote John to George, 'certainly a
pleasant fellow in the main when you are with him
but . . .'

When Clarke took the verses of Keats to show to
Hunt, B. R. Haydon, the painter, who was there, read
them. Haydon was at the peak of his fame, having
brought about the acquisition of the Elgin Marbles
by the British government. It was therefore no slight
compliment to Keats when he asked that the young
man be brought to his studio. In a note to Clarke
dated 31st October John showed his delight:

> *My daintie Davie,*
>   *I will be as punctual as the Bee to the Clover.*
> *Very glad am I at the thoughts of seeing so soon this*
> *glorious Haydon and all his creation.*

It was the fashion in literary circles to write a poem

to fit an occasion and the day after the visit to Haydon's studio, Keats duly sent a letter and a sonnet:

Nov. 20th

My dear Sir —
Last evening wrought me up, and I cannot forbear
sending you the following —
Yours unfeignedly
John Keats. —
Great Spirits now on Earth are sojourning
He of the Cloud the Cataract the Lake
Who on Helvellyn's summit wide awake
Catches his freshness from Archangel's wing
He of the Rose, the Violet, the Spring
The social Smile, the Chain for freedom's sake
And lo! — whose stedfastness would never take
A Meaner Sound than Raphael's Whispering.
And other Spirits are there standing apart
Upon the Forehead of the Age to come;
These, These will give the World another heart
And other pulses — hear ye not the hum
Of mighty Workings in a distant Mart?
Listen awhile ye Nations, and be dumb!
Removed to 76. Cheapside.

This triple tribute to Wordsworth, Hunt and Haydon, started one of the strangest intimacies of Keat's career. Haydon was both a comic and a tragic figure. An intensely religious man who disapproved of Hunt as immoral yet, at first, couldn't resist his fascination, a mediocre painter who dealt only in abnormally

large canvasses to express his exaggerated ideas, a
borrower who believed that the world owed his genius a living and never paid back the loans, he nevertheless did Keats a service with his half mad, inspired
talks. His egotistic faith in his talents could hardly
have failed to spur Keats to develop his own poetical
aims.

Haydon has been described as a 'glorious lunatic'.
He had only to look in the glass, it seems, to realise
that he was a great man. He was, however, undoubtedly a brilliant writer and conversationalist. Keats
certainly owed a debt to Haydon for arousing the
Greek instinct in him. 'Except the blind forces of nature,' declared Haydon, 'nothing lives in the world
which is not Greek in origin'. Explaining the authentic beauty of the Elgin Marbles and the classical inspiration of Raphael's cartoons, which at his instiga-
tion were brought from Hampton Court to London
for exhibition, he started Keats on the search for
beauty and truth.

The relationship between Keats and Haydon is remarkable for its revelation of the younger man's respect for the ideals Haydon represented as well as for
the self sacrificing generosity and patience of the
poet in the face of Haydon's selfishness. Followers of
Keats find it hard to forgive the erratic painter's mad
and untrue account of the poet's drunkenness. It was
sensationalism of the meanest sort, dealing with the

reputation of a dead friend who had shown his wor-
thiness and constant loyalty. Haydon was unreliable,
plainly. One marvels at the fact John put up with him.
He actually wrote more friendly letters to Haydon
than to any other person except his own dear sister.

An entry made in the books of Guy's Hospital listed
John as a dresser to serve twelve months from March
1816. If that is correct, he probably bothered his head
very little with thoughts of medicine after joining the
Hunt circle in November 1816. Poetry was to be the
king henceforth and had been, according to Stephens,
even before he met Hunt. Stephens, who liked to
write verses in bold declamatory style, kept in touch
with his poetically inclined medical friend, probably
until Keats left London to write *Endymion*. From
Stephens's letter to Mathew, part of which has already been quoted, it is evident that John still continued in some fashion to go to the hospital. At any
rate they were seeing each other frequently. Their
friendly companionship included swimming in the
Middlesex New River, visits in the country and meetings at Cheapside.

The spirit of the Vale of Health which so much influenced Keats through association with Hunt, and
his friends gathered there, should have added Shelley
to its benefits when the latter turned up at Hampstead in December 1816, probably to thank Hunt for
his article in *The Examiner* on 'Young Poets'. Some

time in that month Keats and Shelley met at the Vale
of Health cottage. Three years older than Keats, Shelley was a brilliant, headstrong, highly nervous person. He came of an old, distinguished family and
was heir, by entail, to a baronetcy and an income of
£6,000 per annum. He hated restraint of authority
but loved to assist with money those of his fellow men
and women who, in his somewhat erratic opinion,
needed help or persuaded him that they did. Unlike
Keats he had, before they met, lived a hectic and notorious existence, having quarrelled with his father,
been expelled from Oxford and left his wife, Harriet
Westbrook, and his children. Dreamer that he was,
he had a vision of a 'faultless companion' while walking to Horsham, and soon after found her in Godwin's
daughter, Mary Wollstonecraft, who was living, un-
married, with him when he met Keats. His adult life
had been dogged by women, all of whom, it seems,
loved him.[11]

Though Shelley's eager mind probably impinged
on that of the younger man, the two poets never became intimate friends. The difference in their back-
grounds and the impact of Shelley's contradictory
temperament, keen to gain proselytes for his impracti-
cal ideas, were reason enough why Keats failed to res-
pond. However, for two months at Hampstead, they
met frequently and compared notes. In person they
could not have been less alike. Shelley was tall and

thin, with a squeaky voice; Keats was broad shoul-
dered, with a short, compact, well developed stature,
and a voice that has been described as 'rich & low'.
Shelley, who at heart was really generous and kind,
liked Keats and wanted to help him with advice. He
had been urged, as we know, to publish what he had
written but Shelley disapproved. They argued the
matter during walks on Hampstead Heath and even
discussed, it is said, their respective plans of writing
long poems, Keats his *Endymion* and Shelley what
turned out to be *The Revolt of Islam*. When Shelley
found John set on getting into print, he may have
recommended the Olliers, his own publishers, who
brought out Keats's book in 1817.

John gave copies to all his friends, not even forget-
ting his former guardian, old Abbey, who said to Taylor long afterwards:

> He brought me . . . a little Book which he had got
> printed – I took it & said I would look at it because it
> was his writing, otherwise I should not have troubled
> my Head with any such Thing – when we next met I
> said, Well John I have read your Book, & it reminds
> me of the Quaker's Horse which was hard to catch,
> & good for nothing when he was caught – So your
> Book is hard to understand & good for nothing when
> it is understood.

Abbey's opinion seems more brutal but no more

damning than the indifference of the public. Only
two copies sold.

What John may have thought of the failure of his
book to reach the public we do not know. Brother
George, on his own, saw fit to blame the Olliers in
some fashion. A tart reply came from them on 29th
April 1817, after John had left for the Isle of Wight:

> Sir: *We regret that your brother ever requested us
> to publish his book or that our opinion of its talent
> should have led us to acquiesce in undertaking it.
> We are, however, much obliged to you for reliev-
> ing us from the unpleasant necessity of declining
> any further connection with it which we must have
> done ...*

Hot temper seldom pays. Ollier, with whom the Keats
brothers quarrelled is said to have furnished Lock-
hart of *Blackwood's Magazine* with hostile, personal
details of John Keats.

Even before the Olliers actually published his
book, John had decided to choose another firm to act
for him in the future – possibly because he thought
Shelley had too much supervision at the Olliers'. Reynolds had introduced him to John Taylor and James
Hessey who conducted business at 93 Fleet Street,
London, under the name of Taylor and Hessey. As it
turned out Keats was indeed fortunate in having them
as publishers. They kept him in funds 'for the sake of

poetry first and advantage after'. While Hessey man-
aged the business end, Taylor, a man of learning, acted as editor and collaborator of the firm's publications. The quality of mind and critical instinct he
applied to the editing of *Endymion* and the 1820 volume were of considerable value to Keats.

The seventeenth birthday of Tom had come around
on 18th November 1816, with John writing a sonnet
for the occasion addressed 'To my Brothers' beginning:

> *Small, busy flames play through the fresh laid*
>   *coals,*
> *And their faint cracklings o'er our silence creep*
> *Like whispers of the household gods that keep*
> *A gentle empire o'er fraternal souls.*

and ending:

> *This is your birth-day Tom, and I rejoice*
> *That thus it passes smoothly, quietly.*
> *Many such eves of gently whisp'ring noise*
> *May we together pass, and calmly try*
> *What are the world's true joys, – ere the great*
>   *voice,*
> *From its fair face, shall bid our spirits fly.*

This tender poem expressed a longing which fate
denied them. In two short years both his brothers

were to leave John, George to go to America, Tom to
his grave.

In November or December another event of moment to George and John occurred. Georgiana Augusta Wylie, daughter of James Wylie, Adjutant of a
Fifeshire regiment, became a factor in their lives.
George married her eighteen months later and took
her to a pioneer home in Kentucky.

John loved her too, telling her so in a charming
sonnet beginning

> *Nymph of the downward smile and sidelong*
>   *glance,*
> *In what diviner moments of the day*
> *Art thou most lovely?*

'Little George' (a name John gave her) was only fourteen at the time and sixteen when she married. Lov-
ing Georgiana brought John his first serious thoughts
on womankind and caused him to modify his conde-
scending tolerance of them. He must have rather en-
vied his brother. She remained his ideal but C. W.
Dilke, in his annotations to R. M. Milne's *Life and
Letters of John Keats*, described her, with rather ob-
streperous merriment, as 'a pretty, lively, ignorant
girl unaccustomed to Society – more need not be
said . . . She visited England some time after & staid
some short time at my house, & brought with her a
daughter as wild as a red Indian'.

The circumstances that Keats had longed for came to pass in the winter of 1816-17. He could henceforth devote his life to poetry and associate with friends who were interested in the same sort of things. Clarke and Haslam he knew since boyhood days but the others, who were to make up his intimate circle and with whom he discussed poetry, philosophy, life's problems and had fun, he knew for the first time only at the end of 1816 or in 1817. The sequence of their becoming acquainted with him was Severn, Hunt, Haydon, Reynolds, James Rice, Taylor, Hessey, Richard Woodhouse Junior, Charles Wentworth Dilke Junior, Charles Brown and Benjamin Bailey. To these men almost all of his letters (other than those to his sister, his brothers and to Fanny Brawne) were written.

CHAPTER FOUR

THE STRUGGLE OVER ENDYMION:
1817

THE TWO YOUNG POETS Reynolds and Keats had much in common. Their intimate friendship began in 1817. Reynolds, one year older than Keats, was the author of three books and dramatic critic on the newspaper *Champion*. At the time they met, he hoped to win success as a writer of poetry. His love of nature, his gift of criticism and his facility at writing attracted Keats. But Reynolds was no genius; he also lacked the stamina of Keats. Although a witty companion, clever and popular, he failed in the essentials of firm purpose and application. One of his witticisms, however, is worth remembering:

> *Time is a lover of old books and he suffers few new ones to become old.*

Reynolds came under the spell of Miss Eliza Drew, a young Devonshire lady, who persuaded him, as a condition of their marriage, to accept an opening in a law office his friend, James Rice, was able to offer him. The gesture of surrender to Miss Drew which he wrote in *The Garden of Florence,* his last book of serious verse, was both humorous and neatly put:

Thou hast entreated me to write no more,
To turn aside from the consuming art;
And can I shun the voice that I adore
The voice that hath an echo in my heart?
Perchance a gentleman of twenty-four
And upwards should abandon verse in part,
And keep a house, and plunge in tax vexations
And die and leave a Will for his relations.

For about two years Reynolds was the literary con-
fidant of Keats and the recipient of many serious,
worthwhile letters from him touched with fun and
gaiety. They used to lie on the grass at Hampstead
with a book between them discussing poetry and all
the problems of life. This close intimacy lessened materially in 1819, due to absorption of each of them in
separate love entanglements and also to the affection
for Keats developed by Charles Brown of Hampstead
who practically took command of John's existence
after Tom's death in December 1818. Reynolds failed
at law and could not regain momentum as a writer.

When Keats brought out *Endymion* with disappointing results, his friend wrote him 'But I shall set
my heart on having you, high, as you ought to be. Do
you get fame and I shall have it being your affectionate and steady friend'. Reynolds was too easy going
and too fond of Keats to be jealous of his superior
ability.

After his death Reynolds wrote what may truly be

taken as a trustworthy, first hand appraisal of Keats :

*He had the greatest power of poetry in him of any
one since Shakespeare, – He was the sincerest friend
– the most lovable associate – the deepest listener
to the griefs and disappointments of all around him
– 'that ever lived in the tide of time'.*

The year 1817 was advancing and the long poem
based on the love of Endymion for Phoebe, the moon
goddess, which Keats announced he was going to
write, had been thought out but not yet begun. Hunt
and Shelley were hurt, so John believed, because he
did not seek their advice on how to plan it. When
Shelley invited Hunt and him for a long visit to Marlow, he declined, preferring to go alone to the Isle of
Wight to make his own 'unfettered' effort. He explained his situation to Reynolds on 17th March :

*My Brothers are anxious that I should go by myself
into the country – they have been extremely fond
of me, and now that Haydon has pointed out how
necessary it is that I should be alone to improve myself, they give up the temporary pleasure of living
with me continually for a great good which I hope
will follow. So I shall soon be out of Town.*

The plan of *Endymion* which Hunt, and perhaps
Shelley, had criticised, is confused and difficult to
understand. Keats identified himself with a shepherd

F

of Latmus who, apparently in a dream, embraced the moon goddess and caught melancholy moon sickness. He disclosed his predicament to Peona, his imaginary sister. Then he wandered in search of his Phoebe, encountered many subterranean adventures, visited Neptune and his palaces, Bacchus triumphant, and ended by falling in love with the Indian maid he had dreamed about in the story he wrote during the anatomy lesson at Guy's Hospital. The Indian maid turned out to be identical with the immortal moon goddess, Phoebe. It is quite understandable that Professor Lowes remarked in his *Road to Xanadu:*

> *After dipping out of every fountain to which he came, Keats emptied helter-skelter all his brim-filled bowls into* Endymion!

Before taking coach for Southampton from the Bell and Crown in Holborn at four o'clock in the afternoon of 14th April 1817, he purchased a set of Shakespeare in seven volumes (pocket size). On arrival at Southampton, homesick for his brothers, he unboxed his new purchase, writing them that Shakespeare 'comforted' him. He had been reading Shakespeare with Haydon all winter, had inspired his brothers to do likewise and had come, he said, 'very near agreeing with Hazlitt that Shakspeare is enough for us.' Discouraged and humble when contemplating the magnanimous spirit of the Elgin Marbles and the plays of the great bard, he resolved to raise himself if possible to the same level. Two years were to pass before he gained the altitude he sought but 1817 marked the beginning of the climb. The rich intensity and vigour of Shakespeare's poetry remained his ideal to the end.

From Southampton Keats could see the shore of the island on which he hoped to compose his poem. Telling George he was forced to wait until three o'clock for the sailing boat to take him over, he said he felt 'rather muzzy', the result of travelling all night. On landing he explored the island as far as Shanklin and concluded that Carisbrooke was a more central and economical place to live so he engaged a room in Mrs Cook's cottage (now known as Canterbury House) on the road leading to Carisbrooke Castle. Unpacking his books, he wrote to Reynolds that he had found a head of Shakespeare to hang over them. Then pinning up 'Haydon – Mary Queen of Scots and Milton with his daughters in a row', he described the view from the cottage:

> I see Carisbrooke Castle from my window, and have found several delightful wood-alleys, and copses, and quick freshes. As for Primroses – the Island ought to be called Primrose Island: that is, if the nation of Cowslips agree thereto, of which there are diverse Clans just beginning to lift up their heads

*. . . I intend to walk over the Island east – West –
North South . . . I shall forthwith begin my Endymion which I hope I shall have got some way into by
the time you come, when we will read our verses in
a delightful place I have set my heart upon near the
Castle –*

Although Keats began his visit in a cheerful mood,
he became lonely and depressed in Mrs Cook's cottage. He had already invented, according to Stephens, the famous first line of *Endymion* while dreaming poetry in Guy's Hospital. Now, working out the
plan of the poem, arranging the episodes and the allegory, he found composition not so easy. He thought
he would do better in his old lodging at Margate. After only one week at Carisbrooke, he left for Margate
where Tom joined him for company. George, anxious
over his brother's depression, went for advice to Haydon who at once sent John a long letter ending with a
cheering message: 'God bless you, My dear Keats go
on, don't despair, collect incident, study character,
read Shakespeare and trust in Providence – and you
will do – you must, you shall – '
     The letter from Haydon was strong medicine – 'the
shot in the arm' John needed. Perhaps it innoculated
him, for the moment, with a touch of Haydon's gran-
diosity. Keats's reply, however, was modest and only
tentatively grand:

*. . . truth is I have been in such a state of Mind as to
read over my Lines and hate them. I am "one that
gathers Samphire dreadful trade" the Cliff of Poesy
Towers above me . . . I remember your saying that
you had notions of a good Genius presiding over
you. I have of late had the same thought – for things
which [I] do half at Random are afterwards confirmed by my judgment in a dozen features of Pro-
priety. Is it too daring to Fancy Shakespeare this
Presidor?*

Composition went a little better at Margate. As a
town it seems to have been without trees, a lack that
affected John's nerves. On 10th May the brothers
moved to Canterbury where John hoped Chaucer's
influence would set him forward 'like a billiard ball'
and where in fact he did finish the first book of *Endymion.* When Tom returned to Well Walk, Hampstead, to which place George and he had moved
from 76 Cheapside, London, John decided to go to
Hastings for a holiday. At lodgings in Bo-Peep (now
St Leonard's) he could indulge in the relaxations of
a seashore watering place.

His encounter and flirtation there with an unnamed
lady brings up the question of his relations with
women. That Keats wrote sensuous poetry is to his
credit. It accounts for the rich naturalness and emotional appeal of his verse and its tingling effect on his
readers. But sensuality in him may be doubted. Men

of the Georgian era were expected to experience sex before marriage. Women, on the other hand, were classed either as profligate or conventional. Until he exposed himself to the fatigue and rigours of the Scottish adventure and contagion from his dying brother, Keats was strong, vigorous and fullblooded. It is not to be supposed that his occasional erotic verses are meaningless. There may, however, have been only bravado in his boast to Stephens:

> *Give me women, wine and snuff*
> *Until I cry out 'hold enough'*

More important is his remark to Reynolds (to whom he wrote without restraint): 'I did not feel very sorry at the idea of the women being a little profligate'.

But with the exception of certain erotic lapses, Keats was pure in his great poetry and clean in his letters. What did he mean, however, in his letter to Tom from Scotland by saying: 'With respect to women I think I shall be able to conquer my passions hereafter better than I have yet done'? It most likely referred to activities at Teignmouth in 1818 which Tom must have been aware of. He was closer to Tom in temperament than to George and hid no secrets from him. The letters to Reynolds and Rice from Teignmouth with their bawdy verses may explain what John meant in his letter to Tom. Certainly the impulse of sex was in the back of his mind, which is not unnatural. Speaking of bees and flowers in his February 1818 letter to Reynolds John said:

> *The flower, I doubt not, receives a fair guerdon from the Bee – its leaves blush deeper in the next spring – and who shall say between Man and Woman which is the most delighted?*

One biographer, Albert Erlande, thought that 'Keats, as a healthy being, regarded sexual love as the principle of all things'. John may have anticipated Bernard Shaw's prescription for good writing:

> *Sexual experience seemed a natural appetite and its satisfaction a completion of human experience for fully qualified authorship.*[12]

In his first letter to George in America written in October 1818, John disclosed an amorous adventure dating back to 1817 when he was on holiday at Hastings. He said he met by chance near Lamb's Conduit Street in London a 'lady' whom he had known previously ('warmed to' and 'kissed' as he put it) – the same lady, he told George,

> *... whom I saw at Hastings and whom I met when we were going to the English Opera ... She has always been an enigma to me – she has been in a Room with you and with Reynolds and wishes we*

should be acquainted without any of our common
acquaintance knowing it.

That John saw a good deal of the Hastings lady is
shown by his account to George in February 1819:

> ... *the Lady whom I met at Hastings and of whom*
> *I said something in my last I think, has lately made*
> *me many presents of game, and enabled me to make*
> *as many – She made me take home a Pheasant the*
> *other day which I gave to Mrs Dilke; on which, to-*
> *morrow, Rice, Reynolds and the Wentworthians will*
> *dine next door – The next I intend for your Mother.*

Who was this bounteous lady of Hastings that wished
their acquaintance to be kept secret and toward
whom he must have had a sentimental impulse?

Thanks to Robert Gittings, whose *John Keats: The*
Living Year contains scholarly research as to literary
sources that inspired the poet, the mysterious lady
of Hastings is now identified as Isabella Jones. She
turned out later to be a friend and correspondent of
John Taylor, Keats's publisher. Reynolds once referred to her in a letter to Taylor as the 'beautiful Mrs
Jones'. Although at Hastings she was a member of the
household of one Donal O'Callaghan, like herself a
Whig sympathiser, she had an apartment of her own
in London where she received other friends. O'Callaghan was a man about seventy years old and it may

have been with reference to him that Keats wrote the song 'Hush, hush' telling how Isabel hoodwinked her patron. The poem appears to be a jovial recollection of a previous experience with Isabella in which John took part.

I

Hush, hush! tread softly! hush, hush, my dear!
All the house is asleep, but we know very well
That the jealous, the jealous old bald-pate may
     hear,
Tho' you've padded his night-cap — O sweet
     Isabel!
Tho' your feet are more light than a Faery's feet,
Who dances on bubbles where brooklets meet,
Hush, hush! soft tiptoe! hush, hush, my dear!
For less than a nothing the jealous can hear.

II

No leaf doth tremble, no ripple is there
On the river, — all's still, and the night's sleepy
     eye
Closes up, and forgets all its Lethean care,
Charm'd to death by the drone of the humming
     May-fly;
And the moon, whether prudish or complaisant,
Has fled to her bower, well knowing I want
No light in the dusk, no torch in the gloom,
But my Isabel's eyes, and her lips pulp'd with
     bloom.

III
Lift the latch! ah gently! ah tenderly – sweet!
We are dead if that latchet gives one little clink!
Well done – now those lips, and a flowery seat –
The old man may sleep, and the planets may
*   wink;*
The shut rose shall dream of our loves and awake
Full-blown, and such warmth for the morning's
*   take,*
The stock-dove shall hatch her soft brace and
*   shall coo,*
While I kiss to the melody, aching all through!

When he left Hastings in the first week of June
1817, John returned to Hampstead to meet his brothers at the house of Bentley, the village postman, high
up on the hill near the modern Christ Church. Old
Hampstead had a fine situation rambling along a
steep slope with the Heath beside it. Because Tom
was delicate, George moved him there. The Heath
figured prominently in John's enjoyment during his
remaining years of health. It was then 'a stretch of
wild natural country with marshes and bogs, animal
life, wild flowers, wild cherries, pears, crabs and bul-
lace plums in abundance'. John often took his friends
there on exploring excursions, especially Clarke, Reynolds and Severn. Anyone who called at Hampstead
was sure to be introduced to the Heath.

The second book of *Endymion* was finished at

Hampstead during July and August 1817. George
and Tom had gone to Paris leaving John behind. His
work periods were relieved by seeing Clarke, Severn
and his new friends Charles Brown and Charles
Wentworth Dilke Junior to whom Reynolds had introduced him. Hunt had been visiting Shelley at
Marlow and Haydon lived at Lisson Grove in
Middlesex. Browne and Dilke, old schoolfellows, had
built together a two family dwelling, called Wentworth Place, at Hampstead in 1815. Brown was a
bachelor and Dilke a family man with a wife, Maria,
and one son. Keats soon became intimate with the
occupants of both sides of Wentworth Place.

   Brown, a strange mixture of coarseness and decency, warm heartedness and cold blooded calculation,
became a friend devoted to Keats. He sincerely wished to advance John's career, yet was rather jealous of
the latter's more literary minded friends like Reynolds, Dilke and Woodhouse. Dilke who called Brown
'the most scrupulously honest man I ever knew,' said,
nevertheless, he wanted nobleness 'to lift this honesty
out of the commercial kennel'. Although Brown was
kind to John when he couldn't pay his way, he collected from George, after John died, the cost of board
and room with interest added. Brown was given to
horseplay, which Keats also liked. He was grateful to
Brown. 'Without him,' he told his sister, 'I should
have been in, perhaps, personal distress.' Certainly in

his last years Brown was his closest and most intimate associate.

Dilke, a strongly opinionated but just man, devoted to his wife and son, was quite a different sort from Brown. It is therefore not surprising that the Brown-Dilke friendship went on the rocks in the end over differences concerning the Keats family. Maria Dilke, a gay, warm hearted woman, was adored by the Keats boys. She mothered them all, especially Tom. Charles Dilke was a man of considerable mental powers, employed in the Navy Pay Office, Somerset House, when Keats knew him, and later was successful owner and editor of the periodical *The Athenaeum*. At first John saw a good deal of Dilke; he was in the habit of taking his papers and copying them at his house and also studied Milton with him. Dilke, however, did not approve of John's overpowering infatuation for Fanny Brawne. Their intimacy cooled. He had, John thought, 'a sort of parental mania,' was entirely swallowed up in his boy, Charley, and in all things acted as a 'Godwin-methodist'. After John's death Dilke took it upon himself to protect Fanny Keats from her guardian Abbey, and sided with George in America against Brown and Haslam, thus starting the break between Brown and himself.

By midsummer Keats finished the second book of *Endymion*. Meantime Benjamin Bailey had come to London at the beginning of the Oxford long vacation.

He became well acquainted with John, whom he invited to stay at his rooms in Magdalen College. Keats went there on 3rd September 1817. Under the inspiration of Oxford with its venerable traditions, the third book of *Endymion* was written. John had never before visited this ancient college town and lost no time in writing his sister his impressions:

> *This Oxford I have no doubt is the finest City in the world – it is full of old Gothic buildings – Spires – towers – Quadrangles – Cloisters Groves & [c.] and is surrounded with more clear streams than ever I saw together. I take a Walk by the Side of one of them every Evening . . .*

It is pleasant to picture Keats strolling through the gardens and deer park of Magdalen, the most beautiful of Oxford colleges. Magdalen Hall, in which he stayed, now no longer exists. It is referred to by college authorities as the 'old grammar school'.

Bailey described to R. M. Milne in 1849 the ease with which Keats composed at Oxford:

> *. . . he quite acted up to the principle he lays down in the letter of axioms to his publisher . . . 'that if poetry comes not as naturally as the leaves of a tree, it had better not come at all'. This axiom he fulfilled to the letter by his own practice,* me teste, *while he composed the third book of* Endymion, *in the same room in which I studied daily, until he completed it.*

As an earnest student specialising in theology and philosophy, Bailey was good for Keats. He inspired him to make a serious study of Dante's *Divine Comedy* (in Cary's translation), Milton's *Paradise Lost* and Wordsworth's *Excursion* and laid the foundation of his interest in the 'burden of the mystery', a phrase used by Wordsworth in *Tintern Abbey*. With Bailey Keats discussed the philosophical problem of selfishness and disinterestedness or self love and benevolence and his study of Milton, according to Bailey, 'gave him a mighty addition of energy and manly vigour'.

For recreation they went for long walks and punted on the river.

> *For these last five or six days [John wrote to Reynolds] we have had regularly a Boat on the Isis, and explored all the streams about, which are more in number than your eye lashes. We sometimes skim into a Bed of rushes, and there become naturalized river-folks, – there is one particularly nice nest which we have christened "Reynolds Cove," in which we have read Wordsworth and talked as may be.*

On 2nd October they went to Stratford-upon-Avon, to visit the birthplace of Shakespeare. This was a reverend experience for Keats. 'His enjoyment,' Bailey said, 'was of that genuine, quiet kind, which was a part of his gentle nature; deeply feeling what he truly enjoyed, but saying little.' They saw the room in which the great bard was born, went to Holy Trinity Church where he was buried and discussed how closely the monument in the chancel resembled the real Shakespeare.

The wonderful letters John penned to his sister Fanny, George, and his other friends during his remaining two years of vigorous life began on his 1817 visit to Oxford. T. S. Eliot says of them in *The Use of Poetry and The Use of Criticism*:

> *His letters are certainly the most notable and the most important ever written by any English poet.... His letters are what letters ought to be; the fine things come in unexpectedly, neither introduced nor shown out, but between trifle and trifle ... I am tempted into a descant upon the general brilliance and profundity of the observations scattered through Keats's letters ... and their revelation of a charming personality.*

They should be read in detail for their wisdom and humour.

John returned to Hampstead on 5th October to join his brothers. He visited the Reynolds girls, saw Hunt, Haydon and Shelley, also his neighbours in Wentworth Place. He set to work on the fourth and final part of *Endymion*. Ill with a bad cold and cough, he had a false belief in his own condition. He wrote to Bailey: 'The little mercury I have taken has corrected the poison and improved my health . . . Really and truly I do not think my brother's illness connected with mine.'

Because of illness and social interruptions (he composed three or four songs for the entertainment of Jane and Marianne Reynolds) he had finished scarcely more than five hundred lines of the last book of *Endymion* by 21st November. He needed to do five hundred more to complete it. He had grown tired in his long siege of composition.

Anxious to complete his task in a place of stillness and peace he thought of the Fox and Hounds Inn at Burford Bridge between Dorking and Leatherhead in Surrey. Whether Nelson and Lady Hamilton slept at this inn, as claimed, just before the Battle of Trafalgar, I do not know. However that may be, the inn, now greatly enlarged and known as Burford Bridge Hotel, exhibits the rooms of Nelson and Keats, side by side. Most of the garden of 1817 remains, laid out in paths and shrubs with great trees growing against Box Hill which rises precipitously behind the hotel.

> *I like this place very much [Keats wrote in a gossipy letter to Reynolds], there is Hill & Dale and a little River – I went up Box hill this Evening after the Moon – you a' seen the Moon – came down – and wrote some lines.*

And so began the last struggling verses of the poem.
The moon always inspired him. Many times he ap-
pealed to her as representing ideal beauty. On this
night the sight of the young rising moon again stirred
him. He cited her in connection with the flight
through the evening sky of Endymion and the Indian
maid.

   Endymion, as a poem of his youth, is treasured today for its beautiful beginning and bits here and there
such as 'Here lies happiness,' the invocation to Sleep
and the hymn to Pan (Book I): the flight of the butter-
fly – 'Lightly this little herald flew aloft' (Book II):
The song of Sorrow and the cave of Quietude (Book
IV): rather than as a whole. F. T. Palgrave, Professor
of Poetry at Oxford, appraised *Endymion* in a single
apt sentence: 'Splendid as are the foliage and the
flowers, it is an almost pathless intricacy of story – a
paradise without a plan'. Keats himself modestly
joked about this year's work. 'I have most likely,' he
said, 'but moved into the Go-cart from the leading
strings.' In truth *Endymion* is a dream, rampant in
its adolescence, and like a dream confused. John's
friend, Leigh Hunt, made an acute and just review of
the poem, in saying:

   Endymion *it must be allowed, was not a little calcu-
   lated to perplex the Critics. It was a wilderness of
   sweets but it was truly a wilderness, a domain of
   young, luxuriant, uncompromising poetry where*
   G

*'weeds of glorious feature' hampered the petty legs
[of critics] accustomed to the lawns and trodden
walks, in vogue for the last hundred years. . . . Next
to its unpruned luxuriance, the great fault of* Endymion *was the wilfulness of its rhymes.*

Keats had written Reynolds from Carisbrooke: 'I
find that I cannot exist without poetry – without eternal poetry—half the day will not do—the whole of
it – I began with little, but habit has made me a Levi-
athan'. As he looked out at the winter bound side of
Box Hill after finishing *Endymion,* he proved this
statement by composing a song filled with reflective
beauty:

> *In a drear-nighted December,*
> *Too happy, happy tree,*
> *Thy branches ne'er remember*
> *Their green felicity:*
> *The north cannot undo them,*
> *With a sleety whistle through them;*
> *Nor frozen thawings glue them*
> *From budding at the prime.*
>
> *In a drear-nighted December,*
> *Too happy, happy brook,*
> *Thy bubblings ne'er remember*
> *Apollo's summer look;*
> *But with a sweet forgetting,*
> *They stay their crystal fretting,*
> *Never, never, petting*
> *About the frozen time.*

> *Ah! would 'twere so with many*
> *A gentle girl and boy!*
> *But were there ever any*
> *Writh'd not at passed joy?*
> *To know the change and feel it,*
> *When there is none to heal it.*
> *Nor numbed sense to steel it,*
> *Was never said in rhyme.*

By 15th December he was back in Hampstead; George and Tom had gone to Teignmouth in Southern Devonshire for Tom's health.

CHAPTER FIVE

A WINTER OF ADJUSTMENT IN LONDON: 1817-18

◇◇◇

UNTIL HE WENT to join Tom at Teignmouth in March 1818, John was busy revising and copying *Endymion* for the press, writing dramatic reviews for *The Champion*, composing numerous poems, studying Wordsworth and Milton; also going to theatres and to Hazlitt's lectures on 'The English Poets'.

Reynolds, having left for Devonshire in quest of a wife, had asked Keats to take his place for a few weeks in December and January as dramatic critic of *The Champion*. The theatre was an old love. It gave John a free chance to see his favourite actor, Kean, and incidentally to appraise the plays of his hero Shakespeare. Sound criticism of his own poetry and of the works of others was one of the gifts of his genius. He noted how much more Shakespeare delighted, as he himself did, in dwelling upon 'the romantic and wildly natural than upon the monumental'.

In a *Champion* article, he declared that Shakespeare was chained by facts in his historical plays and could not break wildly and at once into the 'breathing fields'.

The poetry of Shakspeare [he said] is generally

free as is the wind – a perfect thing of the elements,
winged and sweetly coloured. Poetry must be free!
It is of the air, not of the earth and the higher it soars
the nearer it gets to its home. The poetry of Romeo
and Juliet, *of* Hamlet, *of* Macbeth *is the poetry of*
Shakespeare's soul – full of love and divine romance.
It knows no stop in its delight but 'goeth where it
listeth' – remaining however in all mens hearts a
perpetual and golden dream. The poetry of Lear,
Othello, Cymbeline, *etc, is the poetry of human pas-*
sions and affections, made almost ethereal by the
power of the poet. Again the poetry of Richard,
John *and the* Henries *is the blending [of] the imagi-*
native with the historical; it is poetry but oftentimes
poetry wandering on the London Road.[13]

During the winter of 1818 John took part in social
affairs more extensively than at any other period of
his life. Being an author and a promising one, at least
in the opinion of his friends, gave him some satisfaction. He had no regrets at leaving the apothecaries.
Though he wrote to Bailey in October 1817, 'I feel from
my employment that I shall never again be secure in
robustness,' he felt keen and alert. In January 1818
he was enjoying the company of his friend James Rice
who, without much health to sustain him, appears to
have been the gayest and best humoured member of
the Keats circle. 'I have had a great deal of pleasant
time with Rice lately,' John wrote his brothers on 5th
January, 'and am getting initiated into a little band

– they call drinking deep dying scarlet . . . they call good Wine a pretty tipple, and call getting a Child knocking out an apple.' Rice always made John laugh. Yet his wisdom more than his wit seems to have impressed Keats who said of him: 'He is the most sensible and even wise man I know. – He has a few John Bull prejudices but they improve him'.

Harmless fooling and spicy Georgian jokes were the order of the day. While health lasted a party with friends was much relished. John dealt out puns with boisterous laughter and carefree enthusiasm. He liked drinking, especially claret.

It fills the mouth one's mouth with a gushing freshness – then goes down cool and feverless – then you do not feel it quar[r]elling with your liver – no it is rather a Peace maker and lies as quiet as it did in the grape – then it is as fragrant as the Queen Bee; and the more ethereal Part of it mounts into the brain, not assaulting the cerebral apartments like a bully in a bad-house looking for his trul and hurrying from door to door bouncing against the waistcoat; but rather walks like Aladin about his own enchanted palace so gently that you do not feel his step.

Keats sometimes took snuff after the fashion of the time and was fond of cards. As a recorder of manners in the days of the Georges, Thackeray had no equal. Card games, then as now, were much in vogue. In

The Virginians, Thackeray mentioned cribbage, all fours, brag, whist, commerce, picquet, quadrille and backgammon as part of the social equipment of his hero. How many of these fashionable games John played we do not know but card playing with his friends and associates brought healthful relaxation from serious composition. On 22nd November 1817 he wrote Reynolds from Burford Bridge: 'Remember me to each of our Card playing Club – When you die you will all be turned into Dice, and be put in pawn with the Devil – '. In at least twelve letters he mentioned cards but never revealed what particular games were in vogue at his card playing club. What were these games? From Scotland John told Reynolds he could not write 'about scenery and visiting' and added 'I will piddle out my information, as Rice says, next Winter at any time when a substitute is wanted for Vingt-un; or perhaps whist was a favourite game at the club. He told Dilke: 'In the Game of Whist if I have an ace I constantly play it first'. The game of loo he knew too. In a letter to Fanny Brawne, he spoke of pam, the knave of clubs, which Pope described in *The Rape of the Lock:*

> *Ev'n mighty Pam that kings and queens oe'r*
> *threw,*
> *And mow'd down Armies in the Fights of Lu,*

And again in February 1818 John wrote to George:

First drawing of Keats by Severn
made at 76 Cheapside in 1816

Original miniature
painted by
Severn in 1819

Profile drawing
given to his sister
in June 1819
'The Head Mr Severn
did of me is now too
dear but here is a
very capital Profile
done by Mr Brown.'

> *Lord! I intend to play at Cut and run as well as Fal-*
> *staff, that is to say, before he got so lusty.*

Probably brag, the ancestor of poker, was the game
played at a party given by Brown and Keats at Hampstead in the spring of 1819 which he described to
George and Georgiana:

> *Yesterday I could not write a line I was so fat[i]gued*
> *for the day before I went to town in the morning*
> *called on your Mother, and returned in time for a*
> *few friends we had to dinner. There were Taylor*
> *Woodhouse, Reynolds – we began cards at about 9*
> *o'Clock, and the night coming on and continuing*
> *dark and rainy they could not think of returning to*
> *town – So we played at Cards till very daylight –*
> *and yesterday I was not worth a sixpence –*

Because John played brag must have been the reason
why Brown wrote to him in Rome, to give him news of
his friends, saying 'the Batch of Brag-players asked
me to town, hoping to fleece me – it was at Reynold's
lodging – and I carried off £2. 10. 0'.

In spite of his love of fun and what Woodhouse, on
one occasion, called 'Keats-like rhodomontade,' John
never let fooling interfere with work. For poetry he
lived impatiently. He had implored his muse in
Endymion:

> *Great Muse thou know'st what prison*
> *Of flesh and bone curbs, and confines, and frets*
> *Our spirit's wings: despondency besets*

> *Our pillows; and the fresh tomorrow-morn*
> *Seems to give forth its light in very scorn*
> *Of our dull, uninspired, snail-paced lives.*

The poems he composed during January and February 1818 included *Lines on Seeing a lock of Milton's hair, On sitting down to read King Lear once again*, a Shakespearian-modelled sonnet celebrating in recollection the charms of his Vauxhall lady beginning 'Time's sea hath been five years at its slow ebb;' the humorous sonnet on Mrs Reynold's cat, the prophetic sonnet 'When I have fears that I may cease to be' and the superb song imitating the repetitive cadences of a thrush in which Keats may have 'consciously translated the wild melody of the thrush into an unrhymed sonnet structure:

> *O thou whose face hath felt the Winter's wind,*
> *Whose eye has seen the snow-clouds hung in mist,*
> *And the black elm tops 'mong the freezing stars,*
> *To thee the spring will be a harvest-time.*
> *O thou whose only book has been the light*
> *Of supreme darkness which thou feddest on*
> *Night after night when Phoebus was away,*
> *To thee the Spring shall be a triple morn.*
> *O fret not after knowledge – I have none,*
> *And yet my song comes native with the warmth.*
> *O fret not after knowledge – I have none,*
> *And yet the Evening listens. He who saddens*
> *At thought of idleness cannot be idle,*
> *And he's awake who thinks himself asleep.*

One of the keenest pleasures he had was attending the lectures of Hazlitt whose 'depth of taste' together with *The Excursion* and Haydon's picture (*Christ's entry into Jerusalem*), Keats had pronounced 'the three things to rejoice at in this Age'. Hazlitt gripped and stimulated his audiences, fixing them defiantly with his large eyes to drive his points home. He hated the existing government of England, which pleased Keats, advocated social reforms and attacked Wordsworth. Keats liked his fiery spirit; 'Hazlitt,' he wrote to Haydon, 'has damned the bigotted and the blue-stockined how durst the Man?! he is your only good damner and if ever I am damn'd – damn me if I shoul'nt like him to damn me'.

During the winter Keats met Wordsworth who with his 'beautiful wife and enchanting sister' was staying with Thomas Monkhouse, a relative by marriage. Haydon described for R. M. Milnes their first meeting:

When Wordsworth came to Town, I brought Keats to him, by his Wordsworth's desire ... Keats expressed to me as we walked to Queen Anne St East where Mr Monkhouse lodged, the greatest the purest, the most unalloyed pleasure at the prospect. Wordsworth received him kindly, & after a few minutes, Wordsworth asked him what he had been lately doing. I said he had just finished an exquisite ode to Pan ... and as he had not a copy I begged Keats

*to repeat it, which he did in his usual half chant
(most touching) walking up & down the room.When
he had done I felt really, as if I had heard a young
Apollo . . . Wordsworth dryly said:*

'*A very pretty piece of Paganism*'.

*This was unfeeling & unworthy of his high Genius
to a Young Worshipper like Keats . . . & Keats felt it
deeply . . .*

Haydon gave a dinner at his studio on 28th December 1817 in honour of Wordsworth. It was called by him 'The Immortal Dinner'. Wordsworth, Lamb, Monkhouse, Edwin Landseer, Joseph Ritchie, Keats and John Kingston, Comptroller of Stamps, were present. Haydon wrote a highly coloured and amusing account of the party.

In spite of the remark about the Hymn to Pan, Keats was polite enough to call on Wordsworth, only to find him on the point of going out to dine, rigged out in full dress, stiff collar, knee breeches and silk stockings, with the Comptroller of Stamps, whom Lamb had ridiculed at the Immortal Dinner. Keats, who was a casual dresser himself, thought him rather foppish, but the great man asked him to dine and Keats accepted. He wrote to Taylor on 10th January, evidently with some pride: 'I have seen Wordsworth frequently. Dined with him last Monday'. He also

told Haydon on 23rd January, 'I have seen a good deal
of WORDSWORTH'. At one of their meetings when
Keats attempted to argue a point, Mrs Wordsworth
remarked 'Mr Wordsworth is never interrupted'. At
heart however, John realised the depth of Wordsworth's thinking and concern for the welfare of mankind.

On 14th February John confided to his brothers:

*I am in the high way of being introduced to a squad
of people, Peter Pindar, Mrs Opie – Mrs Scott – Mr
[Henry Crabb] Robinson, a great friend of Coleridge's, called on me – Richards tell[s] me that my
Poems are known in the West Country and that he
saw a very clever copy of verses, headed with a
Motto from my Sonnet to George – Honors rush so
thickly upon me that I shall not be able to bear up
against them. What think you, am I to be crowned
in the Capitol, Am I to be made a Mandarin—*

Horace Smith, creator with his brother of the famous *Rejected Addresses* which made London laugh
in 1812, invited him to dine. They were considered
genteel society but Keats was not impressed. He said:
'I know such like acquaintance will never do for me'.
He was more at home with Hunt and Shelley in a
rhyming contest, the subject of which was the river
Nile. But 'I am going out too much,' he added.

Keats had gained a definite maturity in this winter

of adjustment. At the very end of it, just before leaving for Teignmouth he wrote his publisher, John Taylor, his famous definition of poetry:

1st. I think Poetry should surprise by a fine excess and not by Singularity – it should strike the Reader as a wording of his own highest thoughts, and appear almost a Remembrance – 2nd. Its touches of Beauty should never be half way ther[e]by making the reader breathless instead of content: the rise, the progress, the setting of imagery should like the Sun come natural natural too him – shine over him and set soberly although in magnificence leaving him in the Luxury of twilight – but it is easier to think what Poetry should be than to write it – and this leads me on to another axiom. That if Poetry comes not as naturally as the Leaves to a tree it had better not come at all.

CHAPTER SIX

TEIGNMOUTH, GEORGE'S MARRIAGE AND SCOTLAND: 1818

IT WAS NOW March 1818. Since he had promised to relieve George who had come to London to arrange his affairs before marrying Georgiana Wylie, John, Devon bound, took fast coach to Exeter, there to change to a slower stage for the rest of the journey. At first Devonshire failed to impress him. He wrote to Bailey: 'Had England been a large devonshire we would not have won the Battle of Waterloo . . . there are vallies of feminine Climate but there are no thews and Sinews'. He had evidently forgotten that men of Devon helped destroy the Spanish Armada.

Teignmouth in the days of Keats was a fishing village in balmy South Devon, situated on a peninsula with sea on one side and a broad tidal river on the other. There are today, as there were in 1818, woods on green hills across the river. Two steep red cliffs, one called the 'Ness' and the other 'Parson and Clerk,' face the sea. Between them lies the town with a fine sandy beach. Although Teignmouth now is a somewhat crowded resort, one can imagine that it had charm in 1818 with pleasant Georgian houses and a wide promenade called the Den, where there was, according to John, always 'music playing'.

Across the street from the house at 20 The Strand, in which Keats's brothers lodged (now marked with a lettered red granite tablet as the residence of John Keats) there stood in 1818 a bonnet shop at number 35 where girls were employed. George had become acquainted with them and this led to the intimacy of the brothers with the Jeffrey family consisting of a widow and four daughters, Marianne, Sarah, Fanny and a small sister who, in John's phrase, 'had a hard brown fist'. John and Tom flirted with the Jeffrey girls who were described as 'lively' and corresponded with them briefly after leaving Teignmouth. The two brothers remained at number 20 until May. Tom's health did not improve; spells of damp wintry weather weighed on them but John, with his ever active humour, made the best of it. He told Bailey:

> ... by the way you may say what you will of devonshire: the thuth is, it is a splashy, rainy, misty, snowy, foggy, haily, floody, muddy, slipshod County – the hills are very beautiful, when you get a sight of 'em – the Primroses are out, but then you are in – the Cliffs are a fine deep Colour, but then the Clouds are continually vieing with them.

The Strand, as it is today, would be a pleasant enough residence in summer. What it must have been like in rainy days or nights of the 1818 winter, living in shut in quarters with a brother who probably coughed tuberculosis germs, can too easily be imagined. *Isabella or The Pot of Basil*, which John wrote at Teignmouth, expressed his sensitive reaction to environment and the plight of poor Tom. He mourned with Isabella over her pot of basil and 'her murder'd man'.

Hazlitt, in a lecture at which John was present, had remarked that the story of Isabella by Boccaccio was worth the attention of a modern writer. After John settled himself at Teignmouth he undertook to interpret the tale, rather in the manner of Chaucer. For some reason he never liked the result, calling it 'too smokeable' and a 'weak-sided poem,' but Reynolds, a keen critic, assured him it had 'that simplicity and quiet pathos which are of sure sovereignty over all hearts'. Charles Lamb, also, considered *Isabella* one of Keats's best poems and Robert Browning thought so well of it that he used to quote the three stanzas, in which Lorenzo, Isabella's lonely lover, talks to her from beyond the grave, as an example of Keats's 'supreme mastery of language'.

Illness in one form or another cast its shadow over John Keats. Besides his tender love for Tom, he was physically affected by illness in others. Like Shakespeare, he had the power of projecting imaginatively his own personality into another's existence. He could, he once said, even take part in the life of a sparrow and peck about the gravel. The insight by which he

H

yielded to the suffering and mood of Isabella in *The Pot of Basil* were instinctive with him. In his first letter from Teignmouth John told Reynolds his reaction against the illness of other persons in no uncertain terms:

> *I intend to cut all sick people if they do not make up their minds to cut sickness – a fellow to whom I have a complete aversion, and who strange to say is harboured and countenanced in several houses where I visit - he is sitting now quite impudent between me and Tom – He insults me at poor Jem Rice's – and you have seated him before now between us at the Theatre – when I thought he look'd with a longing eye at poor Kean. I shall say, once for all to my friends generally and severally, cut that fellow or I cut you.*

Though John at Teignmouth still felt well and vigorous, depressed only by Tom's sickness but keen himself to scour the Devon countryside on all fair days, he was soon to experience progressive illness in himself.

In spite of weather, uncertainty and worry over Tom, he evidently liked Devon and probably found some lively companions there. On the very next day after complaining to Bailey about Devonshire, as already stated, he wrote to Haydon:

> *I have enjoyed the most delightful Walks these three*

fine days beautiful enough to make me content here
all the summer could I stay.

His letters from Teignmouth are spirited and full of
wisdom. Devon spurred him into a productive mood.
The 'Four seasons' sonnet and the lyrics composed in
lighter moments took on an Elizabethan quality. His
passion for knowledge appeared in the 'Homer' sonnet with its splendid beginning 'Standing aloft in
giant ignorance'.

> *I have written to George [he wrote to Reynolds] for*
> *some Books – shall learn Greek, and very likely*
> *Italian – and in other ways prepare myself to ask*
> *Hazlitt in about a years time the best metaphysical*
> *road I can take. For although I take Poetry to be*
> *Chief, [yet] there is something else wanting to one*
> *who passes his life among Books and thoughts on*
> *Books – I long to feast upon old Homer as we have*
> *upon Shakspeare, and as I have lately upon Milton.*

John had already told George: '. . . a little change
has taken place in my intellect lately . . . Nothing is
finer for the purpose of great productions than a very
gradual ripening of the intellectual powers'. At last
he had grown to realise the meaning of the words he
wrote in *Sleep and Poetry:*

> *A nobler life*
> *Where I may find the agonies, and strife*
> *Of human hearts.*

'Chameleon poet,' he called himself; and his vola-
tile, emotional nature readily ran up scale into gaiety
or down into depression. The poem written at Teignmouth for Reynolds, to cheer him through an illness,
had its bright as well as sombre side:

> Dear Reynolds, as last night I lay in bed,
> There came before my eyes that wonted thread
> Of Shapes and Shadows and Remembrances,
> That every other minute vex and please:
> Things all disjointed come from North and south,
> Two witch's eyes above a Cherub's mouth,
> Voltaire with Casque and Shield and Habergeon,
> And Alexander with his Night-cap on –
> Old Socrates a tying his cravat;
> And Hazlitt playing with Miss Edgeworth's cat;
> And Junious Brutus pretty well so, so,
> Making the best of's way toward Soho. . . .
> O that our dreamings all of sleep or wake
> Would all their colours from the Sunset take:
> From something of material sublime,
> Rather than shadow our own Soul's daytime
> In the dark void of Night. . . .
>   . . . It is a flaw
> In happiness to see beyond our bourn, –
> It forces us in Summer skies to mourn,
> It spoils the singing of the Nightingale.

It was at Teignmouth that Keats developed his
'burden of the Mystery' philosophy. He sketched for
Reynolds his idea of this Wordsworthian theory that,
he thought, they both should adopt:

. . . axioms in philosophy are not axioms until they
are proved upon our pulses: We read fine things but
never feel them to the full until we have gone the
same steps as the Author. – I know this is not plain;
you will know exactly my meaning when I say, that
now I shall relish Hamlet more than I ever have
done – Or, better – You are sensible no Man can set
down Venery as a bestial or joyless thing until he is
sick of it and therefore all philosophizing on it
would be mere wording.

and went on to describe his well-known 'Mansion'
with its 'thoughtless' chamber and 'chamber of
Maiden-Thought,' arriving at which 'We feel the
"burden of the Mystery," To this Point was Wordsworth come, as far as I can conceive when he wrote
Tintern Abbey'. Most of his correspondence was addressed to Reynolds and before leaving Teignmouth
to attend George's wedding and prepare for the walking tour in Scotland, John sent Reynolds the winged
words of the lovely *Ode to Maia.*

Mother of Hermes! and still youthful Maia!
        May I sing to thee
As thou wast hymned on the shores of Baiæ?
        Or may I woo thee
In earlier Sicilian? or thy smiles
Seek as they once were sought, in Grecian isles,
By Bards who died content on pleasant sward,
Leaving great verse unto a little clan?
O give me their old vigour, and unheard,

Save of the quiet Primrose, and the span
Of Heaven and few ears
Rounded by thee my song should die away
Content as theirs
Rich in the simple worship of a day. –

When the brothers returned to Hampstead in early
May, illness still cast its shadow. An infected throat
kept John in the house for two weeks. He complained
that night air was bad for him. He wrote to Bailey on
10th June: 'I am not certain whether I shall be able to
go on my Journey [to Scotland] on account of my
brother Tom and a little indisposition of my own'. He
did not realise the import of his recurring sore throat
which under the strain of writing *Endymion* had first
begun to affect him. His stamina and determination
to succeed in what he wanted to do, kept him going
until almost the end of his life.

Although his 1817 volume had received no public
recognition, he was not discouraged. In spite of loss
of parents and his homeless existence, their effect had
been offset by the wise choice of his school, by the
affection of his brothers and by his ability to make
and hold friends. Moreover he had a clear purpose to
gain fame even if it had to be posthumous. 'Life must
be undergone,' he wrote to Bailey, 'and I certainly de-
rive a consolation from the thought of writing one or
two more Poems before it ceases.' In this mood he

seemed really confident and self reliant. Yet he con-
fessed: 'I feel no spur at my Brothers going to America
and am almost stony-hearted about his wedding'.
George was his 'best friend'. 'I have two Brothers,' he
added, 'one is driven by the "burden of society" to
America the other, with an exquisite love of Life, is
in a lingering State.' When the ocean had separated
him from George and when six months later Tom
died, John was left with only a little sister whom a
stubborn guardian kept practically hidden from him.
To these losses fate was to add the adversity of malicious criticisms of himself and the scurrilous attacks
on *Endymion* by the Scottish reviewers.

Meantime, in no spirit of adversity, the wedding
of George and Georgiana had taken place. The bride
and groom escorted by brother John and jovial Charles
Brown left London on Monday 22nd June 1818 for
Liverpool whence the emigrant couple were to sail
for Philadelphia. On the way to Liverpool the coach
stopped for dinner at Redbourne near St Albans.
Henry Stephens, who had settled there as surgeon
apothecary, came to see them and learned for the
first time that Keats had abandoned medicine. Leaving the newly married pair at the Crown Inn in Liverpool to await the sailing of their ship, John and
Charles bade them Godspeed and went on to Lancaster by coach to begin their walking trip.

Brown, an indefatigable walker who made a prac-

tice of spending his days each summer on the road,
had planned this tour of Scotland, hoping Keats would
go with him. At first John thought he had better stay
at home to study literature and philosophy. He had
grown to the point of realising that whatever talent
there was in him craved fulness and not mere luxuriance in expression. In the end the charm of the mountains and Scottish scenery seduced him. He explained
the reason to Bailey: 'I should not have consented to
myself these four Months tramping in the highlands
but that I thought it would give me more experience,
rub off more Prejudice, use [me] to more hardship,
identify finer scenes load me with grander Mountains,
and strengthen more my reach in Poetry, than would
stopping at home among Books even though I should
read Homer'. Tom's doctor told him it was all right
to leave his ailing brother. Another holiday was even
suggested for the invalid himself, who thought it was
possible he might again go to Paris. One wonders if
tuberculosis could have been recognised as serious
in 1818.

The route from Lancaster to Gretna Green on the
Scottish border leads through Kendal and Keswick,
between which towns lies the Lake Country. As the
travellers approached Bowness, Lake Windermere
was spread out before them against the rugged elevation of peaked mountains. It was the first time Keats
had seen a mountain except a glimpse of distant

Welsh landmarks on the way to Liverpool. He ex-
claimed to Brown, 'There is no view in the world to
beat it,' and to Tom he wrote: '. . . the two views we
have had of [Windermere] are of the most noble
tenderness – they can never fade away – they make
one forget the divisions of life; age, youth, poverty
and riches; and refine one's sensual vision into a sort
of north star which can never cease to be open lidded
and stedfast over the wonders of the Great Power'.
Brown and he, in high spirits, crowned the day by
reading aloud on the shore of beautiful Lake Windermere the *Pot of Basil*.

They planned to call on Wordsworth the next day
at his home, Rydal Mount, near Grasmere. On the
way they viewed the waterfall at Ambleside. The call
was a disappointment because all the Wordsworths
were away from home. The best Keats could do was
to leave a note for the great man which he placed over
Dorothy's portrait. Eager to reach Carlisle where
there would be letters awaiting them, they hurried on.
Having walked 114 miles in five days they straggled
into Carlisle with aching thighs and blistering feet.
They were glad enough to take coach for Dumfries
well over the border of Scotland. Although Brown
could claim to be partly Scottish by descent, neither
of them had ever been in Scotland before. To their
amazement they found themselves in a foreign country, with foreign ways and almost a foreign language.

Charles Brown and John had great fun together, joking at each other's expense. Brown teased his companion, writing to Dilke that Keats had been 'abusing the Scotch and their country for five hours, saying thank Providence he is not related to a Scot nor in any way connected with them – the women have such large splay feet'. Brown also described himself to Dilke:

> *Imagine me an odd fellow, and moreover an odd figure: – imagine me with a thick stick in my hand, the knapsack on my back, 'with spectacle on nose,' a white hat, a tartan coat and trowsers, and a Highland plaid thrown over my shoulders. Don't laugh at me . . .*

Keats, in his turn called Brown 'The Red Cross Knight' and declared Brown's shadow was ready to split its sides as it followed him. But John's own costume must have been equally ludicrous, dominated by a battered fur cap which he was still wearing when he arrived at Mrs Dilke's house in Hampstead. Appreciating his own absurdity he wrote to Mrs Wylie from Scotland:

> *When I come into a large town, you know there is no putting one's Knapsack into one's fob; so the people stare. We have been taken for Spectacle-venders, Razor-sellers, Jewellers, travelling linen-drapers, Spies, Excisemen, and many things else I have no*

*idea of. When I asked for letters at the Post Office,
Port Patrick; the man asked what regiment?*

The first serious impression of Scotland on Keats,
however, was an intense reaction to Burns and his
'miserable' lot. He had been stirred by thoughts of
this homely poet of Scotland and his humanities since
he saw his tomb at Dumfries. He wrote to Reynolds:
'One song of Burns's is of more worth to you than all
I could think of for a whole year, in his native country'. No doubt he was humming as he wrote:

> *From scenes like these old Scotia's grandeur
>   springs,
> That makes her loved at home, revered abroad.
> Princes and Lords are both the breath of Kings.
> An honest man's the noblest work of God.*[14]

Two poets have given their impressions on ap-
proaching Ayr, the birthplace of Burns, – Keats from
on foot, Wordsworth from the top of a coach. Keats
said in his letter to Reynolds:

> *... on a sudden we turned a corner upon the imme-
> diate Country of Ayr ... I had no Conception that
> the native place of Burns was so beautiful – the Idea
> I had was more desolate, his rigs of Barley seemed
> always to me but a few strips of Green on a cold hill
> – O prejudice! it was rich as Devon ... Besides all
> the Beauty, there were the Mountains of Arran Isle,*

*black and huge over the Sea – We came down upon
every thing suddenly – there were in our way, the
"bonny Doon", with the Brig that Tam O'Shanter
crossed – Kirk Alloway, Burns's Cottage and then
the Brigs of Ayr – First we stood upon the Bridge
across the Doon; surrounded by every Phantasy of
Green in tree, Meadow, and Hill.*

Wordsworth, more lyrical than Keats on this occasion, paid tribute to Burns's love of nature in a charming sonnet:

> *'There,' said a stripling pointing with meet pride
> Towards a low roof with green trees half-
>   concealed,
> 'Is Mosgiel Farm; and that's the very field
> Where Burns ploughed up the daisy.' Far and
>   wide
> A plain below stretched seaward, while descried
> Above sea-clouds, the Peaks of Arran rose;
> And, by that simple notice, the repose
> Of earth, sky, sea, and air was vivified.
> Beneath 'the random bield of clod or stone'
> Myriads of daisies have shone forth in flower
> Near the lark's nest, and in their natural hour
> Have passed away; less happy than the One
> That, by the unwilling ploughshare, died to
>   prove
> The tender charm of poetry and love.*[15]

Until the end of July when fatigue overcame him,

Keats got keen pleasure out of Scotland. In his first
letters to Tom he communicated his enthusiasm; and
for his sick brother's amusement described Scottish
dancers who

> . . . *kickit and jumpit with mettle extraordinary, and
> whiskit and friskit, and toed it and go'd it, and
> twirl'd it and wheel'd it, and stamped it, and sweated
> it, tattooing the floor like mad; The difference be-
> tween our country dancers and the Scottish figures
> is about the same as leisurely stirring a cup o'Tea
> and beating up a batter-pudding.*

He boasted to Tom: 'I think we are the luckiest fellows in Christendom'. But luck proved a fickle jade
when in August he became 'too thin and fevered to
proceed'. In large part due to the strenuous pace set
him by Brown, who was tireless, John wasted his
vitality on the hills and highways of Scotland. He
had little resistance left to combat the germs of tuberculosis.

From Dumfries, the first place the wayfarers
stopped in Scotland on 1st July, they tramped all the
way to Inverness, covering the Burns country, as already mentioned, 'skudded over to Donaghdee' in
Ireland as far as Belfast, then back to Glasgow. Next
they went to Loch Lomond and Loch Awe, then to
Oban and over to the Island of Mull and Staffa,
climbed Ben Nevis with great difficulty, ending the

tour so far as Keats was concerned at Inverness.
Brown wrote on 7th August to Dilke:

> *We came out to endure and to be gratified with
> scenery and lo! we have not been disappointed either
> way . . . Mr Keats however is too unwell for fatigue
> and privation. I am waiting here to see him off on
> the smack for London. He caught a violent cold in
> the Island of Mull which far from leaving him, has
> become worse and the physician here thinks him too
> thin and fevered to proceed on our journey. It is a
> cruel disappointment. We have been as happy as
> possible together. Alas! I shall have to travel through
> Perthshire and all the countries round in solitude.*

Fatigue did not stop John from writing an account
of their tour to Mrs Wylie, Georgiana's mother (part
of which has already been quoted), probably so that
she could send it to her daughter and George:

> *I have been* werry *romantic indeed, among those
> Mountains and Lakes. I have got wet through day
> after day – eaten oat-cake, and drank Whisky,
> walked up to my knees in Bog, got a sore throat,
> gone to see Icolmkill and Staffa, met with whole-
> some food, just here and there as it happened; went
> up Ben Nevis, and – N.B., came down again. Some-
> times when I am rather tired, I lean rather languish-
> ingly on a Rock, and long for some famous Beauty
> to get down from her Palfrey in passing, approach
> me with – her saddle bags and give me – a dozen or*

two capital roast beef Sandwiches – . . . Besides rid-
ing about 400, we have walked above 600 Miles, and
may therefore reckon ourselves as set out.

The sea trip to London revived Keats somewhat
and he arrived at Hampstead on 18th August as brown
as a berry. Tom's condition shocked him. He had
never received a letter sent by Dilke telling him Tom
had suffered a serious relapse. Writing at once to his
sister he said: 'I shall ask Mr Abbey to let me bring
you to Hampstead'. The recalcitrant guardian added
much to the difficulty of the situation and Tom's emotion on her leaving, whenever his sister was allowed
to come, increased it. Battalions of trouble besieged
John in this time of sorrow. They were reinforced by
the dastardly attack upon him and his *Endymion* by
Scottish journals which were published in August
1818. Such was the power of criticism by *Blackwood's*
that John's whole year's work had been practically
wasted, so far as sale of the book was concerned. He
had hoped it would bring in much needed money.

How philosophically he took criticism was revealed
in a letter Hessey wrote to Taylor on 16th September
1818. It gives, too, a little vignette of Keats and his
prospects:

Keats, Hazlitt, Percival, Woodhouse, and the two
Falkners made up my party on Monday and I be-
lieve they were all well pleased, though I thought

the evening hung a little sometimes . . . Keats was in good spirits. He slept here and stayed some time next morning. He does not seem to care about Black-wood, he thinks it is so poorly done, and as he does not mean to publish anything more at present he says it affects him less. . . . He is studying closely, re-covering his Latin, going to learn Greek and seemed altogether more rational than usual . . . but he is such a man of fits and starts he is not to be depended on. Still he thinks of nothing but poetry as his being's end and aim, and sometime or other he will, I doubt not, do something valuable.

CHAPTER SEVEN

A FATEFUL AUTUMN: TOM'S DEATH: 1818

EARLY IN OCTOBER, 1818, Hessey sent John two letters (printed in *The Morning Chronicle*) which criticised the Scottish attack and pointed out 'beauties of
the highest order' in *Endymion*. Writing in reply to
Hessey John said:

> *I begin to get a little acquainted with my own
> strength and weakness. – Praise or blame has but a
> momentary effect on the man whose love of beauty
> in the abstract makes him a severe critic of his own
> Works. My own domestic criticism has given me
> pain without comparison beyond what Blackwood
> or the Quarterly could possibly inflict, and also when
> I feel I am right, no external praise can give me such
> a glow as my own solitary reperception & ratifica-
> tion of what is fine. . . . That it is [slipshod] is no
> fault of mine. – No! – though it may sound a little
> paradoxical. It is as good as I had power to make it
> – by myself.*

In conversation with the poet at Hessey's party in
September, Woodhouse, anxious as always for Keats's
success, got the impression that John said he would
write no more. When the second attack was printed
in *The Quarterly Review*, Woodhouse wrote John a

I

long letter begging him to reconsider, which brought
in response his definition of a poet:

> *A Poet is the most unpoetical of anything in exist-*
> *ence; because he has no Identity — he is continually*
> *. . . filling some other Body — The Sun, the Moon, the*
> *Sea, and Men and Women who are creatures of im-*
> *pulse are poetical and have about them an unchange-*
> *able attribute — the poet has none; no identity — he*
> *is certainly the most unpoetical of all God's Crea-*
> *tures. . . . It is a wretched thing to confess; but is a*
> *very fact that not one word I ever utter can be taken*
> *for granted as an opinion growing out of my identi-*
> *cal nature — how can it, when I have no nature?*

His 'no identity' theory grew out of thinking over
the assertion of Hazlitt, made in the lecture on the
English Poets that John heard in February 1818:

> *The striking peculiarity of Shakespeare's mind was*
> *its generic quality, its power of communicating with*
> *all other minds — so that it contained a universe of*
> *thought and feeling within itself; and had no par-*
> *ticular bias, or exclusive excellence more than an-*
> *other. . . . He was least of an egoist that it was*
> *possible to be. He was nothing in himself; but he*
> *was all that others were or that they could become.*
> *. . . He had only to think of anything to become that*
> *thing, with all the circumstance belonging to it . . .*
> *the poet may be said, for the time, to identify him-*
> *self with the character he wishes to represent, and*
> *to pass from one to another. . . . His characters are*

real beings of flesh and blood; they speak like men
not like authors. One might suppose that he stood
by at the time, and overheard what passed.

To this quality in Shakespeare John gave the name
– 'Negative Capability, that is, when a man is capable
of being in uncertainties, mysteries, doubts without
any irritable reaching after fact and reason'. According to Keats the mind of such a man should be a
'thoroughfare for all thoughts'. It should be made up
about nothing at all. Since thinking of nothing at all
was equivalent to thinking of all manner of things, it
followed that the mind should spread its facets to reflect the shine of any ideas fancy found attractive.

Lovers of the poet owe a debt to Richard Woodhouse. As literary advisor to the firm of Taylor and
Hessey he probably kept active their interest in Keats
in spite of his vagaries. Woodhouse had all published
volumes of the poems interleaved to record notes and
comments on their contents. He preserved in a Book
of Transcripts and a Commonplace Book, letters,
anecdotes and unpublished poems, also every varia-
tion of text obtained from any source. He accurately
appraised the poems as early as October 1818 in a
letter to his cousin Mary Frogley:

Such a genius, I verily believe, has not appeared
since Shakespeare & Milton: and I may assert with-
out fear of contradiction from anyone competent to

judge, that if his Endymion *be compared with
Shakespeare's earliest work written about the same
age, Keats's poem will be found to contain more
beauties, more poetry (and that of a higher order),
less conceit and bad taste and in a word much more
promise of excellence than are to be found in Shakespeare's work. — This is a deliberate opinion: nor is
it merely my own.*

The spirit behind his interest is revealed in a noble
sentence he wrote to Taylor: 'Whatever people regret
that they could not do for Shakespeare or Chatterton,
because he did not live in their time, that I would em-
body into a Rational principle and with due regard to
certain expediencies do for Keats'. Woodhouse also
sent John a letter of appreciation written by Jane
Porter, the author of the well known *Scottish Chiefs*,
which he was too modest to quote in full to his brother George. It said 'such true parnassian fire – always
burns its brilliant way thro' every obstacle'.

In November John received a letter marked 'If not
delivered return to P. Fenbank P.O. Teignmouth'. It
contained a flattering and complimentary sonnet ending with a promise of help.

> *And there is one whose hand will never scant
> From his poor store of fruits all* thou *canst want.*

The sentiment was better than the poetry but the
letter also contained a £25 note. Of this anonymous

gift he wrote to George: '... the present galls me a little – and I do not know whether I shall return it if I ever meet with the donor – after whom to no purpose I have written'. More serious troubles faced him in the autumn of 1818 than attacks on *Endymion* and anonymous gifts. The brother he loved was slipping away from him. Caring for Tom day and night, watching his suffering and rapid decline were painful details of existence, brightened only by a new light of friendship in the person of Fanny Brawne.

During this autumn Keats reached a turning point in his development as a poet which caused him to change his thinking. The first element was the stimulation of his vision due to his Scottish tour. It brought him freedom from care in the stirring atmosphere of Scotland and formed a salient angle to his earlier experiences. The background of mountains, lochs and islands helped him to adopt finally the objective, empirical manner of Shakespeare. He was to turn to Shakespeare and Milton from the humanitarian philosophy of Wordsworth which he described to Reynolds from Teignmouth; from benevolence to the principle of beauty in all things and to the sublime rather than the simple. The philosophy of Wordsworth had not in his experience solved the problem of living. His best friend and brother had left him to settle in America. Poor Tom, too, was in a 'lingering state'. Henceforth imagination (the principle of negative capability) which he believed could be more real than reality, was to be his consolation and his guide.

Undoubtedly a second element in the change must have been the attack on Keats in the Scottish reviews and the indifference of the public toward his long labour in creating his egotistical poem *Endymion.* He lost faith in the good intentions he himself sought to sound forth and in human nature as a whole. The final element which completed the change was his falling really in love. The sublimation of his thoughts into pregnant words of controlled emotion, which appeared in his great poems after meeting Fanny Brawne, made those poems great. Strong excitement and exhilaration caused by his reading Chapman's *Homer* with Cowden Clarke in 1816 had, to be sure, intuited a masterpiece but its equal could not have been matched and surpassed without the sustained inspiration of his philosophy of negative capability.

He refused Severn's offer to relieve him at night in caring for Tom. More and more he suffered from contact with sickness. 'I wish I could say Tom was any better,' he wrote to Dilke; 'His identity presses upon me so all day that I am obliged to go out - and although I intended to have given some time to study alone I am obliged to write, and plunge into abstract images to ease myself of his countenance his voice and feebleness — so that I live now in a continual fever — it must be poisonous to life although I feel well.'

The 'abstract images' were no less than those that finally became the grand epic *Hyperion*. He had begun to plan this story of the Titans in September 1817, had reflected on it during the Scottish tour which supplied some of the background, and now worked intermittently on it while tending Tom. The demands on him of his brother's last days forced laying it aside. Tom was so nervous that he could not speak to him. John warned George the end was near: 'I cannot even now ask him for any Message – his heart speaks to you – Be as happy as you can – Think of me and for my sake be cheerful.' And of the end which came on 1st December 1818 he wrote: 'The last days of poor Tom were of the most distressing nature; but his last moments were not so painful and his very last was without a pang'.

In his grief Keats turned to Brown who has told how he was awakened in bed by the touch of a hand:

It was Keats who came to tell me that his brother was no more. I said nothing, and we both remained silent for a while, my hand fast locked in his. At length, my thoughts returning from the dead to the living, I said 'have nothing more to do with those lodgings, – and alone too! Had you not better live with me?' He paused, pressed my hand warmly, and replied – 'I think it would be better'. From that moment he was my inmate.

Worn out with nursing, nervous and deep in sorrow, John was in all probability unbalanced for a short time. At Wentworth Place, which bordered on the open heath, small wild animals would sometimes invade the garden. One day in early December Dilke shot a rabbit. Keats declared it to be the spirit of his dead brother returning to him. The demonology he had learned from Mary Tighe's *Psyche* and Wieland's *Oberon*, from which he adopted imagery, may have convinced him in his delirium that spirits are free to wander, even to return, as he believed was the case with poor Tom's.

The period between Tom's death and John's proposal to Fanny Brawne was one of confusion and longing. Deeply in love with her, John was uncertain about the outcome. He seems to have been bewildered. He let Brown accept for them both an invitation to spend Christmas in Hampshire, and at the same time he agreed to dine with the Reynolds family at their home in Little Britain. When later Mrs Brawne asked him to spend Christmas at her house – the invitation he really longed for – he excused himself at Little Britain because of a previous engagement in Hampshire. Meantime he had sent Brown off to Hampshire to explain that a sore throat kept him in London. By his awkward apology to Mrs Reynolds, he made a mess of it but, no doubt, Fanny Brawne was worth a little chicanery!

CHAPTER EIGHT

FANNY BRAWNE AND ISABELLA JONES

WHILE THERE may have been indications of dalliance on the part of John Keats, he never fell seriously in love until Fanny Brawne came into his life in 1818. Her arrival within the Keats circle (as soon as her place in it was realised by his friends and followers) resulted in acrimony concerning her that lasted more than a century. With Mary Frogley and other conventional young ladies, he appears to have made a frolic out of their relationship, sharing the association usually with his brothers. The Mathew sisters, the Reynolds unit and the Jeffreys of Teignmouth, were treated as family groups.

The jocular attitude towards them and his deprecating thoughts towards women in general underwent a change after he came to love Georgiana Wylie and accept her as George's wife. Knowing her was a spiritual revelation. Shortly before George's marriage he wrote Bailey a letter in which he sought to define real or ethereal things, one of which he called:

Things semi-real such as Love, the Clouds &c which require a greeting of the Spirit to make them wholly exist . . .

His ideas on love and marriage are reflected in his correspondence from Scotland after he said goodbye to the young married couple on their way to America and was still thinking of them. He wrote to Reynolds from Maybole in July:

> ... now one of the first pleasures I look to is your happy Marriage — the more, since I have felt the pleasure of loving a sister in Law. I did not think it possible to become so much attached in so short a time. Things like these, and they are real, have made me resolve to have care of my health ...

A little later in the same month, he wrote to Bailey from Inverary:

> When I was a Schoolboy I though[t] a fair Woman a pure Goddess, my mind was a soft nest in which some one of them slept, though she knew it not – I have no right to expect more than their reality ... I never rejoiced more than at my Brother's Marriage and shall do so at that of any of my friends – ... I could say a good deal about this [his 'obstinate Prejudice' against womankind in general] but I will leave it in hopes of better and more worthy dispositions – and also content that I am wronging no one, for after all I do think better of Womankind than to suppose they care whether Mister John Keats five feet high likes them or not.

Plainly he was hoping to meet the perfect type like

Georgiana. He found it, in his opinion, on his return from Scotland. He was ripe for love.

There was much in Fanny Brawne to attract a strongly sexed man like Keats. She was small, about his height – an important point since he was sensitive on his stature. Though not conventionally beautiful, she was unusual looking. Her eyes were a brilliant blue and she wore blue ribbons in her hair to match them. She 'knew the value of elegance,' had taste in her dress, her smile was disarming and her voice 'singularly sweet'. With an attractive figure, a very soft, white skin and her ready acceptance of his admiration, she must have seemed very desirable. Dreaming of her later, he used such phrases as:

Cheek-pillowed on my Love's white ripening breast

and, again,

Let none else touch the just new-budded flower.

When thoughts and dreams of possessing Fanny became an obsession with Keats his friends naturally deplored the attraction, but, rather unjustly, took a dim view of her. Reynolds, at one time his closest friend, called her 'the poor idle thing of woman-kind, to whom he has so unaccountably attached himself'. But another male, Gerald Griffin, who met Fanny in 1825, four years after Keats's death, wrote his sister a more unbiased opinion:

Keats you must know was in love and the lady he
was to have married . . . is a beautiful young crea-
ture . . . sadly changed and worn, I thought, but still
most animated, lively and even witty in conversa-
tion. She quite dazzled me in spite of her pale looks.

Fanny's wit and repartee were well known in Hampstead society.

The date when John and Fanny first saw each other
has never been fixed. It is, therefore, of some interest
to consider the events that followed the occupancy
of Wentworth Place by the Brawne family. Brown
and Keats had left for Scotland on Monday 22nd
June 1818. Since the wayfarers expected to be gone
on a four months' 'pedestrian tour through the north
of England and Scotland as far as John O'Grots,' Mrs
Brawne's tenure was probably for four months until
the middle of October. She was a well-to-do widow
with three children, Fanny, the eldest, Samuel and
Margaret. The Dilkes were at that time occupying
the larger side of the same house, the two parts of
which were separated by a thin partition wall and
were surrounded by a garden used in common. To
anyone visiting Keats House today it must be clear
how intimately associated the occupants of the two
sides could be and probably were. The Dilkes and
Brawnes became friends at once. If anyone called at
the Dilkes', the Brawne family could hardly fail to
know it and vice versa.

Leaving Brown in Scotland to continue the tour by himself John arrived at Hampstead on 18th August. Mrs Dilke who saw him that evening sent the news to her father in law:

> John Keats arrived here last night, as brown and shabby as you can imagine; scarcely any shoes left, his jacket all torn at the back, a fur cap, a great plaid and his knapsack. I cannot tell what he looked like.

and Mr Dilke, so John wrote to his brother, was also at home on his arrival:

> I found him, Dilke, very ailing on my return – he was under medical care for sometime and then went to the Seaside . . .

After her husband departed, Mrs Dilke remained at Wentworth Place at least until 22nd September (John proposed going to town with her on that day) and Dilke returned to Hampstead before his wife left for her holiday.

The intimacy of the Keats boys with the Dilkes was of long standing. John had been invited to their house before he went to the Isle of Wight to begin writing *Endymion* in March 1817. Since early spring of that year the brothers who then moved to Well Walk, Hampstead, had been welcome at Wentworth Place. Dilke afterwards wrote proof of this to Severn:

At that time [1817] Brown and myself lived in adjoining cottages at Hampstead, and the Keats John, George and Tom, were with me three times a week, often three times a day.

After George left for America and John for Scotland in June 1818, both Mr and Mrs Dilke were solicitous in their attention to Tom. As soon as he began alarmingly to fail, the doctor insisted that his brother should be sent for, and Dilke wrote to John to come home. Meantime Mrs Dilke had heard through Brown that John was already giving up the walking tour and returning. She wrote again to her husband's father at Chichester:

I am rather glad of it as he will not receive the letter which might have frightened him very much as he is extremely fond of his brother.

There can be no doubt of the active concern of Mr and Mrs Dilke in the welfare of the whole Keats family. Knowing this, John on his arrival naturally called at once at Wentworth Place and probably repeated his visits from day to day. Dilke wrote many years later that John was there 'every day'. It is inconceivable to me that two young people coming or going to and from Wentworth Place could have avoided seeing each other at some time between 18th August

and October 1818, even if Mr and Mrs Dilke failed
to introduce them, which was unlikely.

There are four good reasons for identifying an earlier date of their meeting than has been previously
considered. Fanny Brawne is a reliable witness of
events in her own life. On 18th September 1820, she
wrote to John's sister:

> *I have known your brother for two years – am a*
> *great friend of Mrs Dilke.*

There is confirmation of this statement, hitherto not
commented upon, to indicate that Fanny was accurate in saying 'two years,' meaning at least two years
before 18th September 1820. Fanny explained her
association with John Keats to Thomas Medwin who
was preparing to write a life of Shelley. In the *Life*,
Medwin quoted from her letter written in answer to
his inquiry:

> *I did not know Keats at the time the review [The*
> *Quarterly Review] appeared . . . [He] started on a*
> *walking expedition into the Highlands. From thence*
> *he was forced to return, in consequence of the ill-*
> *ness of a brother, whose death a few months after-*
> *wards affected him strongly . . .*

Following this quotation Medwin went on for three
pages of his book to other matters, and on the fourth
page he continued quoting from Fanny's letter:

It was about this time, continues my correspondent,
that I became acquainted with Keats. We met fre-
quently at the house of a mutual friend (not Leigh
Hunt's) but neither then nor afterwards did I see
anything in his manner to give the idea that he was
brooding over any secret grief or disappointment.
His conversation was in the highest degree interest-
ing, and his spirits good, excepting at moments when
anxiety regarding his brother's health dejected them.

A reasonable inference from this letter is that John
and she met 'about the time' of his return from Scotland and that they were intimate long before Tom
died on 1st December 1818.

Secondly, the fact that John had begun by September to cogitate the subject of love, as possibly involv-
ing himself, raises a suspicion that some sort of mental change, a positive jolt in fact, must have occurred
to inspire him to quote Ronsard to Dilke on 21st September:

'Love poured her Beauty into my warm veins.' You
have passed your Romance and I never gave into it
or else I think this line a feast for one of your lovers...

and on the following day to congratulate Reynolds,
for the second time, on his forthcoming marriage:

Indeed I am grieved on your account that I am not
at the same time happy — [why on his account?] but

MY DEAR REYNOLDS,

Believe me, I have rather rejoiced at your happiness than fretted at your silence. Indeed I am grieved, on your account, that I am not at the same time happy. But I conjure you to think, at present, of nothing but pleasure ; " Gather the rose," &c., gorge the honey of life. I pity you as much that it cannot last for ever, as I do myself now drinking bitters. Give yourself up to it—you cannot help it —and I have a consolation in thinking so. I never was in love, yet the voice and shape of a woman has haunted me these two days—at such a time when the relief, the feverish relief of poetry, seems a much less crime. This morning poetry has conquered—I have relapsed into those abstractions which are my only life—I feel escaped from a new, strange, and threatening sorrow, and I am thankful for it. There is an awful warmth about my heart, like a load of Immortality.

Poor Tom—that woman and poetry were ringing changes in my senses. Now I am, in comparison, happy. I am sensible this will distress you—you must forgive me. Had I known you would have set out so soon I would have sent you the " Pot of Basil," for I had copied it out ready. Here is a free translation of a Sonnet of Ronsard, which I think

will please you. I have the loan of his works—they have great beauties.

" Nature withheld Cassandra in the skies,
For more adornment, a full thousand years ;
She took their cream of Beauty's fairest dies,
And shaped and tinted her above all Peers :
Meanwhile Love kept her dearly with his wings,
And underneath their shadow filled her eyes
With such a richness that the cloudy Kings
Of high Olympus uttered slavish sighs,
When from the Heavens I saw her first descend,
My heart took fire, and only burning pains,
They were my pleasures—they my Life's sad end ;
Love poured her beauty into my warm veins,
[So that her image in my soul upgrew,
The only thing adorable and true.—Ed.] *

―――――――

* The second sonnet in the " Amours de Cassandre : " she was a damosel of Blois—" Ville de Blois—naissance de ma dame."

" Nature ornant Cassandre, qui denoit
De sa douceur forcer les plus rebelles,
La composa de cent beautez nouvelles
Que dés mille ans en espargne elle auoit.—
De tous les biens qu' Amour au Ciel couuoit
Comme vn tresor cherement sous ces ailles,
Elle enrichit les Graces immortelles '
De son bel œil qui les Dieux esmouuoit.—
Du Ciel à peine elle estoit descenduë
Quand ie la vey, quand mon ame esperduë
En deuint folle, et d'vn si poignant trait,
Amour couler ses beautez en mes veines,
Qu' autres plaisirs ie ne sens que mes peines,
Ny autre bien qu' adorer son portrait."

Dilke's comment on Keats's letter
pertaining to Fanny Brawne
*By courtesy of the Pierpont Morgan
Library, New York*

I conjure you to think of nothing but pleasure
"Gather the rose &c" – Gorge the honey of life. I
pity you as much that it cannot last for ever, as I do
myself now drinking bitters. – Give yourself up to it
– you cannot help it – and I have a consolation in
thinking so. I never was in love – yet the voice and
the shape of a Woman has haunted me these two
days . . .

Then he went on to say that 'Poetry' had conquered
and he had 'relapsed into those abstractions which
are my only life'. But he had to admit:

There is an awful warmth about my heart like a load
of Immortality. Poor Tom – that woman – and Poe-
try were ringing changes in my senses.

The combination of time, place and opportunity
seems to force a conclusion that the 'shape and voice'
haunting Keats from September 1818 were those of
Fanny Brawne. It is, of course, understandable that
Harry Buxton Forman when editing the letters of the
poet should have considered 'that woman' to be the
cousin of the Reynolds sisters, called by Keats 'Charmion,' she being the only person mentioned with admiration in the poet's letters at a date anywhere near
September 1818 and it was only natural that writers
on Keats since then should have accepted, without
further thought, Forman's dictum.

It will be observed, however, whereas *in October*

K

John dismissed Charmion with the casual remark 'she kept me awake one Night as a tune of Mozart's might do — I speak of the thing as a passtime and an amuzement,' and also seized the opportunity to give his sister in law a deft compliment on her ability to save him from worldly women; *in September* he had expressed to Reynolds a much deeper and quite different emotion about the three things that really mattered to him. Grouping 'that woman' with poor dying Tom whom he dearly loved and Poetry whose 'abstract images' topped his life gave her a permanence in his mind Charmion never possessed.

In the third place, it is noteworthy that neither R. M. Milnes in his *Life, Letters and Remains of John Keats* nor Charles Wentworth Dilke in annotating it, appears to have thought of Charmion when commenting on 'that woman' mentioned in the 22nd September letter to Reynolds. In the text immediately following quoting the letter, Milnes had this to say:

> *It may be as well at once to state that the lady alluded to in the above pages inspired Keats with passion that only ceased with his existence. Where personal feelings of so profound a character are concerned, it does not become a biographer, in any case, to do more than indicate their effect on the life of his hero . . .*

And Dilke, in his comments about the letter on the

identical page the letter was printed on, in the copy
of Milnes's book (now in the Morgan Library, New
York), wrote:

> *About this time, he met Miss Brawne for the first*
> *time at my house. Brown let his house when he &*
> *Keats went to Scotland to Mrs Brawne, a stranger to*
> *all of us. As the house adjoined mine, in a large*
> *garden, we almost necessarily became acquainted.*
> *When Brown returned, the Brawne's took another*
> *house at the top of Downshire Hill; but we kept up*
> *our acquaintance & no doubt Keats who was daily*
> *with me met her soon after his return . . .*

Lastly, Andrew Lang, called 'the bookworm of his
age,' arbiter of literary matters in the nineteenth century, who still holds a unique position in the literary
world, in commenting on the poet in his *Letters on
Literature* (1889) wrote:

> *What a good fellow Keats was. How really manly*
> *and in the best sense, moral he seems, when one*
> *compares his life and letters with the vagaries of*
> *contemporary poets . . .*

and, after noting that Keats said the voice and shape
of a woman haunted him and that he had sent Reynolds a letter dated 22nd September 1819, enclosing
the *Ode to Autumn*, added this observation:

> *This was the last of his published letters to Reynolds.*

*He was dying haunted eternally by that woman's
shape and voice.*

Whatever the date of first meeting Fanny Brawne
may have been, John quickly surrendered to her
charms. Thought of her was much in his mind from
that moment. He told her later:

> the very first week I knew you I wrote myself your
> vassal; but I burnt the Letter as the very next time I
> saw you I thought you manifested some dislike to
> me. If you ever feel for a Man at first sight what I
> did for you, I am lost.

He dearly loved his brother, however, and his time,
energy and affection were actively devoted to caring
for Tom until the end. Nevertheless it is unfortunate
he dissembled his love affair to the extent he did. Instead of being secretive about his overwhelming admiration for Fanny and commanding her never to let
his name cross her lips, indeed if he had publicly admitted his love in normal fashion, he might have light-
ened the load of sorrow and disappointment in his
life. But perhaps genius, spurred by illness, in Thomas Mann's phrase, is never normal! Keats would then
probably have himself dated and dedicated to Fanny
his poem entitled *Ever let the fancy roam;* and 'pleasure' would have remained 'at home'. There can be
little doubt that Fanny inspired this poem and also
the first version of the 'Bright Star' sonnet, both of

which are supposed to have originated in Keats's mind during the early autumn of 1818.

> *O the Ravishment — the Bliss!*
> *Fancy has her there she is —*
> *Never fulsome, ever new,*
> *There she steps! And tell me who*
> *Has a Mistress to [for so] divine?*

Now that the hitherto mysterious lady Keats met at Hastings in May 1817, has been identified by Robert Gittings as Isabella Jones, an interesting question has been raised. How high is she to be rated in the emotional and creative life of the poet? Mr Gittings is her discoverer and naturally a partisan. He is, however, frank in saying in the Foreword of his book:

> *A new story, such as this, . . . may only reflect a personal taste and an opinion of the moment.*

Quite arbitrarily, I think, Mr Gittings sweeps aside the possibility that Keats had met Fanny at Wentworth Place soon after his return from Scotland on 18th August 1818, (as Dilke said he did) and had fallen in love with Fanny on first meeting her (as Keats said he did).

Isabella Jones, if one can infer anything from her background and experience, must have been older than Keats. Let us see her as Mr Gittings has described her:

*She was certainly beautiful; she was specially re-
membered nearly twenty years later by Reynolds,
an expert in such matters, as 'beautiful Mrs Jones,'
and she sat this winter for her portrait by A. E.
Chalon, which appeared in the Royal Academy exhibition of 1819. She was in the habit of spending
her summers in or near Hastings with an elderly,
irascible, and apparently rich Irishman named Mr
Donal O'Callaghan; there is no mention of any Mr
Jones. She wintered in London, and was very hos-
pitable. She prided herself on giving parties where
one could meet pretty women and sensible men, and
where the sensible men could show their good sense
by looking at the pretty women. Her case of liqueurs,
which Keats noticed, contained some of the choicest
Scotch whisky, and wherever she went she seems to
have been able to command expensive and well furnished lodgings. She had a lively, not to say a biting
wit, and she wrote an excellent style. Her literary
tastes were those fashionable in her day; she read
novels of the Gothic 'horror' type – the counterpart
of the modern thriller – popularized by Mrs Ann
Radcliffe, and was interested in the poetry of Barry
Cornwall. She was a particular intimate of Taylor,
and seems to have shared in the gatherings of the
brilliant coterie the publisher assembled when he
edited the London Magazine in the early 1820s . . .*

 *Probably at the time of Keats's death, Richard
Woodhouse added this note to the copy of* The Eve
of St Agnes *which he had made in his MS Book:*

 St Agnes day is the 21st of January.

*The Poem was written on the suggestion of Mrs
Jones.*

*Isabella was just the person to have suggested such
a poem. Keats later spoke of* The Eve of St Agnes *as
a poem written on a popular superstition; Isabella's
letters show her to have been well acquainted with
such superstitions, especially those relating to friendship and love . . . Woodhouse knew her well enough,
either now or later, to set her down without question
as the inspirer of the poem. It seems likely enough
that she suggested it to Keats on the very night of
the legend, January 20th, when he visited her before
his journey south . . . Just as the 'Hastings lady' of
Keats's letters is one and the same as 'Mrs Jones' of
Woodhouse's note, so the mysterious tale is the same
as the poem. The lady and the story are intimately
mixed; for it was the legendary subject, suggested
by Isabella Jones, which brought Reynold's suggestion from Boccaccio into life and poetry in Keats's
excited brain.*

*Isabella Jones may have brought it to life in a very
particular sense. Keats spent the night of January
20th, St Agnes Eve, in Town before catching the
early-morning coach to Chichester. On January 21st
he wrote the lyric recounting the successful love-
affair with Isabella, and started writing* The Eve of
St Agnes. *In the latter poem, Keats insisted that the
love-affair between his hero and heroine on St Agnes
Eve was actually consummated . . .*

*Keats was a normal young man of his time in many
ways, in spite of being 'a very odd young man' in*

others. Extraordinary as his gifts were, he was young
enough and ordinary enough to make, only a few
days later, the usual youthful pun on the name of
the place where he was going to stay, about a young
woman 'here in Bed-hampton'. In his 'rhodomon-
tade' about the offending passages in St Agnes, he
said, according to Woodhouse, 'that he should des-
pise a man who should be such an eunuch in senti-
ment as to leave a maid, with that Character about
her, in such a situation'. If such a situation presented
itself to him on the evening of January 20th - as we
may believe by the lyric it did - it is at least possible
that he lived up to his words.

Possible? – Yes – for Keats had mentioned in his
letter to George of 18th February 1819, that he was
seeing frequently the 'lady whom I met at Hastings'.
I surmise, however, Mr Gittings's purpose in painting
Isabella Jones as bed companion of the poet, is to justify his argument that she so inspired Keats by her
sexual charm that he had her in mind when he wrote
both the first draft of the 'Bright Star' sonnet in October 1818, and *The Eve of St Agnes* in January 1819.
His argument seems to be overworked. Many of his
inferences are not supported in the notes – for instance, he gives no authority for the flat statement
that Keats visited Mrs Jones on the night of 20th January 1819, before setting out for Chichester. John may
have enjoyed his pleasures like many other young
men but no one can claim that he put Isabella on a

pedestal to be worshipped as he did Fanny Brawne.

Mr Gittings has, I think, failed to recognise the integrity of John Keats, who was most forthright and honest in his use of words, when he ignored John's statement concerning Isabella Jones made in October 1818, in the letter to his brother:

> I have no libidinous thoughts about her – she and your George are the only women à peu près de mon age whom I would be content to know for their mind and friendship alone.

Hasn't Mr Gittings interpreted the October letter to George out of focus? It was the first letter John wrote to his brother in America. It was a calm letter. There was nothing in it to indicate any excitement on John's part. He said:

> I intend to write you such Volumes that it will be impossible for me to keep any order or method in what I write: that will come first which is uppermost in my Mind, not that which is uppermost in my heart – besides I should wish to give you a picture of our Lives whenever by a touch I can do it; ...

Later in the same letter he described his chance encounter with the 'lady met in Hastings' in 1817. By any standard John certainly wrote without excitement but Mr Gittings, building up his case for Isabella's emotional hold on Keats, has used such misleading phrases as the following:

> *He re-opened his letter to George, in a state of great excitement, to chronicle an adventure. . . .*
>
> *. . . An experience and emotion which at this very time occupied the whole of Keats's being. . . .*
>
> *. . . These intense feelings, both on love and on poetry, had been brought to the surface by his meeting with Isabella Jones. . . .*
>
> *. . . Keats returned the same way back to Holborn, in the same excited state, and with, as he so expressively put it, his 'guessing at work,' as well it might be, about the beautiful and enigmatic companion at his side. . . .*
>
> *. . . during the weekend of October 24th-25th, when he was so deeply stirred by his meeting with Isabella Jones.*

However partisan anybody can be in support of the emotional role Mrs Jones played in Keats's life, it must be admitted that he met and knew of Fanny Brawne's existence before Tom died. He evidently could not resist telling his brother George about her in his letter of mid-December. He spent Christmas Day with her, cancelling two previous commitments elsewhere, dined again on New Year's Day 1819, at the Brawnes' and probably put off, on her account, going to join Brown at Chichester until late in January.

John's statement to George that his Hastings lady friend and Georgiana were the only women he would be content to know 'for their mind and friendship alone' sufficiently explains Isabella's literary interest in his writings. It is significant that he puts her in the same class with George's wife. To suggest a legend to an author, as a subject to write about, is not a 'libidinous' act; neither does it, necessarily, give an author the inspiration and personal experience from which a great poem is born.

Fanny's statement to John's sister that Christmas Day 1818, spent in her brother's company, had been the happiest she had then spent, and the fact that John had obviously been seeing a good deal of Fanny before Christmas, rather belittle Mr Gittings's unrealistic explanation that Christmas 'was probably the first occasion on which he came alone to her house, and she was able to see him as himself, without the company of the Dilkes or Brown'. In fact a careful reading of *John Keats: The Living Year* seems to me to reveal so many inferences deduced from unsubstantial incidents in the poet's life that it is not surprising to find a review of the book in *The Observer* of London under the date of 17th January 1954, saying:

Mr Gittings would have proved more if he had not tried to prove so much, and many of the literary correspondences he discovered are convincing only if we wish to find them so . . .[Isabella's] age . . . does not suit the line:

> *Cheek-pillowed on my Love's white ripening breast.*

We would have to know much more about Mrs Jones before attributing to her the inspiration for that line.

CHAPTER NINE

BEDHAMPTON: A VERIFICATION
1819*

◊◊

AMY LOWELL, principal American biographer of
Keats, inserted in the second volume of her life a
photograph of The Towers at Bedhampton with the
caption that it was the house in which Keats spent his
last night in England. Talking with Mr J. H. Preston,
Assistant Curator of Keats House at Hampstead, one
day in the summer of 1951, I remarked that it seemed
unlikely John Snook, the farmer and miller, whom the
poet visited in 1819 and again in 1820 just before sailing for Italy, had lived in such a large and imposing
mansion, more suited to be the home of so called 'carriage folks'.

In the joint letter Keats and Brown wrote on 24th
January 1819, from the Snook house to Charles and
Maria Dilke at Hampstead, Brown poked fun at an
old friend, saying:

*Old Dicky has not called during my visit, – I have
not seen him; the whole of the family are* shuffling

---

* The substance of this chapter on Bedhampton was
published in *The Keats-Shelley Journal* Vol III 1954
page 1.

to carriage folks for acquaintances, cutting *their old friends and dealing out pride & folly, while we allow they have got the* odd trick *but dispute their* honours.

Writing from The Towers Brown would hardly have made such an observation.

Encouraged by Mr Preston, who thought the identity of the house should be established, if it still existed, I decided to explore Bedhampton. Before going I wrote to Mr Frank R. Byerley, who, Mr Preston told me, now lived at The Towers. He most courteously replied that he believed a John Snook had died in his house when it was known as Belmont Castle. He added, however, that his friend, Captain B. R. Willett, CBE, DSC, RN (Ret.), tenant of the Old Mill House at Bedhampton, told him that John Snook whom Keats visited had, according to local tradition, lived in the Old Mill House.

To see the house (if I could) where the poet had actually been inspired to compose *The Eve of St Agnes* seemed to me very well worth while and I wrote to Captain Willett who graciously responded by inviting me to inspect the house and to stay for luncheon. Captain Willett and his young son, George, met me at Havant (the station for Bedhampton) and we motored towards the foreshore to the border of an extensive marsh that stretches to the waters of Langstone Harbour. Near the house we went over railway tracks by a remarkable bridge composed of thirteen arches.

The Mill House was situated on the far side of a small stream crossed by a narrow bridge. At my first glimpse I saw a Georgian house surrounded by dense, tall trees. It made a charming picture. The ground floor of the house included a hall, an ample living room, a dining room and the usual service offices. Mrs Willett greeted us; Mr Byerley also had come for luncheon; we sat down, perhaps in the same room where Brown ate breast of muir fowl after Keats and he arrived from Chichester. Captain Willett said the only change in the original house is a modern kitchen he himself added. After luncheon he showed me a stone tablet cut in a wall of the house which read:

The gift of Mr George Ridge at Sublington Farm in Portsea Island in memory of his very good friend George Champ Senior June 30 1742.

We talked of Keats and of his visit in 1819. After the death of Tom Keats on 1st December 1818, John went as already stated, to live with Charles Brown at Wentworth Place. Brown was intimate with all the Dilke family and it was arranged that Brown and Keats should spend Christmas with Charles's sister, Letitia, and her husband, John Snook, who lived at Bedhampton. Keats did not, however, join Brown at Chichester until the middle of January 1819. The reason usually given for this is that he remained at

Hampstead because of his love for Fanny Brawne. John himself said it was because of a sore throat. Another possible reason is that he was trying to raise money for his artist friend B. R. Haydon, who was as usual in difficulties. The exact date the poet left London is not recorded but it could not have been later than Wednesday 20th January 1819, for he wrote to George in America that he spent 'a few days at old Mr Dilke's, going out twice to "old Dowager card parties" '.

Brown was visiting old Mr Dilke, Charles's father, at a house in Hornet Square, Chichester, (11 Eastgate Square). The old dowagers, whose card parties John mentioned, were probably Miss Mullins and Mrs Lacy. The game they played was loo. The visit to Chichester certainly ended on Saturday 23rd January. On that day, Brown and Keats walked twelve miles to Bedhampton arriving at the Snook house at three o'clock too late for dinner. They were in high spirits and sent off the joint letter, already mentioned, dated Sunday 24th January, full of puns, to the Dilkes at Hampstead.

On Monday they made a day's journey to Stansted to attend the consecration of the chapel in Stansted Park built or adapted by a wealthy barrister named Way as part of a college for the conversion of the Jews. It was an excursion of curiosity on their part, for the hobby of Mr Way was much talked of,

The Old Mill House, Bedhampton
photograph by Captain B. R. Willett

and they took Mr Snook's young son John, 'the boy', with them. This visit gave Keats ideas of architecture and decorations which he used in *The Eve of St Agnes.*

Brown returned to Hampstead the next day. Keats, who was not very well, remained at Bedhampton. When he returned home in February he described his visits:

> *I was nearly a fortnight at Mr John Snook's and a few days at old Mr Dilke's—Nothing worth speaking of happened at either place—I took down some of the thin paper and wrote on it a little Poem call'd 'St. Agnes Eve'...I said nothing of consequence happened at Snook's—no more than this that I like the family very much Mr & Mrs Snook were very kind—we used to have over a little Religion and politics together almost every evening—and sometimes about you—He proposed writing out for me all the best part of his experience in farming to send to you ...*

The Old Mill House is noteworthy in the life of Keats because of the unusual charm of its setting as well as for its possible effect on his work. Mrs Willett pointed out its compelling influence when she said: 'It has been our home for so many years and has a dreamlike quality which is hard to explain. I have lived here alone a great deal and I can well understand how Keats sensed its enchantment with his sen-

L

sitive mind'. John indicated in his letter to George that he was happy at Bedhampton. The beauty of the simple old place must have stirred him, artist that he was, to compose his great poem sublimating the intensity of the love he felt for Fanny Brawne into the romance of his hero Porphyro who, in the imagination of the poet, played the part he himself longed to play. St Agnes Eve (21st January) had just gone by. John was in the mood to blend the old legend and incidents of his own life into the astonishing events of the great poem.

In spite of the sore throat which kept him in poor health, he must have written thirty or forty lines of poetry each day – poetry comparably more mature and finished than any work he had hitherto produced except *On First Looking into Chapman's Homer*. John Keats also slept at the Old Mill House on his last night in England. On Thursday 28th September 1820, the brig *Maria Crowther* on which Joseph Severn and he were, lay becalmed in Portsmouth harbour. They went to Bedhampton to call on Mr and Mrs Snook and stayed for the night. The brig left Portsmouth the next day, Friday, on its way to Naples.

It is a strange fact that the Old Mill House has never been described in any life of Keats. Captain Willett told me he had never inquired into the tradition that Keats had visited his house. I employed

through his co-operation, Bruton & Birkett, solicitors,
115 High Street, Portsmouth who, at my expense, prepared a brief of the title and history of the house. I am
therefore able to verify the Old Mill House as the residence of Keats's friend John Snook, and also to give a
brief résumé of the Snook family. Three generations
touched the life of the poet. They were John Snook I,
merchant of Portsea, who bought the Old Mill House;
John Snook II, the friend of Keats; and John Snook
III, 'the boy,' who also had an older brother Henry.

John Snook I was a merchant doing business in
White's Row and St George Square, Portsea Island.
He probably was contractor to the Navy. The Mill
House and other buildings and land at Bedhampton
were purchased by him, then described as of Portsea
in the County of Southampton Merchant, by deed of
Conveyance dated 5th April 1797 made between
James Champ, the elder, and James Champ, the
younger, of the one part and John Snook of the other
part. The Bedhampton Mill property may have been
bought for the benefit of John Snook II, the son of
John Snook I. At any rate the son was living at Bedhampton in 1804. In the *Hampshire Telegraph and
Sussex Chronicle* for Monday 26th November 1804,
there appeared an announcement of his marriage:

Havant – Marriages
On Monday Mr J. Snook of Bedhampton to Miss

Dilke, daughter of C. W. Dilke, Esqre. of the Navy Pay Office, London.

John Snook I made his will dated 13th July 1819, whereby he devised and bequeathed the Mill House, Bedhampton and other lands and premises (all stated in the said will to be in the occupation of his son, John Snook) to his said son (John Snook II) his heirs and assigns for ever. John Snook I died at his residence in St George Square Portsea, on 19th July 1819. In the *Hampshire Telegraph and Sussex Chronicle* for Monday 26th July 1819, the following notice appeared:

> *Died on Monday evening last at his residence in St George Square, Portsea, in his seventy-seventh year deeply lamented, Mr John Snook, an eminent Merchant of that town. He was a man of real worth and unaffected piety.*

The official land tax returns of Bedhampton are lodged in the Hampshire office at the Castle, Winchester, Hants, and were produced by the County archivist.

The land tax return for the year 1819 reads *(inter alia)* as follows:

Owner	Property	Occupier
Mr Jno. Snook	Mill House and land	Himself
		£10 15s 6½d

The land tax return for the year 1821 reads *(inter alia)* as follows:

Owner	*Property*	*Occupier*
Mr Jno. Snook	Mill House and land	Himself
		£9 5s 6½d

The return for 1820 was not available. A visit to the burial ground at Bedhampton Old Church revealed the records of the members of the Snook family who resided in Bedhampton. Cut on the tombstones are their dates:

John Snook born Oct. 7, 1780, died Jan. 29, 1863
Letitia Snook born Apr. 1, 1784, died Mch. 9, 1865
Henry Snook born Oct. 1, 1805, died June 8, 1879
John Snook [the boy] born June 2, 1807, died Feb. 1, 1887
Mary Augustus Snook [wife] born May 1, 1808, died May 19, 1878

Henry and John Junior are dim figures in the Keats circle. There are several existing letters addressed 'Master Henry Snook at Mr Lord's Academy, Tooting, Surrey' from Brown who took an interest in him. 'The boy' survived all the others and was known as the 'Master Baker.' He died in 1887 at The Towers, Bedhampton.

On 18th July 1849, John Snook II made his will whereby he devised and bequeathed *(inter alia)* all his water corn mill situate in Bedhampton and also all his messuage or dwelling house connected with said mill, described as being in the occupation of his sons, to his sons Henry Snook and John Snook Junior for the benefit of his wife Letitia Snook during her life and after her death equally between Henry Snook and John Snook Junior.

The Reverend H. P. Stokes, MA, Rector of the Parish Church of St Thomas, Bedhampton, published in 1918 a book entitled *Bedhampton* setting forth the local tradition of the Old Mill House. On page 35 the following statement is inserted:

THE OLD MILL HOUSE

. . . is a very pretty property, remarkable for a brief visit of the poet Keats to his friend the Master Baker, MR SNOOK.

It came about in this way: he was becalmed in Portsmouth Harbour. Finding he would be unable to sail that night, he rowed to shore at Bedhampton with his friend, and spent the night in England with MR SNOOK.

It was supposed to have been at one time a Priest's House, for the Old Mill here joins the Upper Mill. There is a cupboard – now removed to Mr Stirling Stent's House – arranged to serve men from, and afterwards closed if need be. Here were the old ovens . . . where the biscuits were baked for the Crimean soldiers. MR SNOOK, the Master Baker, made his fortune in this Mill, and left a large portion of it to the late SIR CHARLES DILKE, Bart, his nephew[16] who refused it, and sold it to MISS

MEIKLAM. MR SNOOK died at The Towers, Belmont Hill, and is interred in Bedhampton Churchyard.

CHAPTER TEN

HAMPSTEAD: THE TOP OF SOVEREIGNTY: 1819

IT IS IMPOSSIBLE now to identify the landmarks in Enfield and Edmonton connected with Keats, because they have been obliterated by the growth of a great city, but the actual surroundings in which he lived at Hampstead, Teignmouth, Bedhampton, Chichester and Winchester and became inspired to write some of his most beautiful poems, still exist. Of these Wentworth Place at Hampstead (now known as Keats House in Keats Grove) is the most important. It became his principal residence from 1st December 1818, until he left for Italy in September 1820. There one can visualise him against a background that seems stamped with his personality. There he struggled to bind closer his love ties with Fanny Brawne, dreamed the calm of *The Eve of St Mark*, the irony of *La Belle Dame Sans Merci*, created all the Odes except *Ode to Autumn*, and ended his golden period with the completion of the two 'Hyperions'. In spite of its being somewhat crowded by the modern museum and library building on the same lot, Wentworth Place with its garden, in which he often sat composing, has a nostalgic charm for lovers of the poetry of John Keats.

For some years following the poet's death, Wentworth Place was occupied by persons who loved him and knew him well – by Mrs Brawne and her family until her death in 1829 and by his sister Fanny Keats after her marriage to Senor Llanos, a Spaniard, until 1831 when she moved to Spain. In 1838 the house was bought by Miss Eliza Chester, an actress of unusual beauty who had attracted the attention of the Prince Regent. She later became Court Reader to him as King. Miss Chester converted the two separate units into a single dwelling and added the present Chester Room. At the same time the name of the house was changed to Lawn Cottage and later became known as Lawn Bank.

The house had many different tenants after 1840 and its identity with Keats became lost. Towards the end of the nineteenth century, however, when the house was being repainted, workmen found under old paint the words 'Wentworth Place' over the door of Dilke's separate entrance. Fortunately Dilke had placed the name there as a tribute to distinguished ancestors. A circular plaque was put over this door in 1895 by the Hampstead Literary and Antiquarian Society with the inscription:

John Keats

Poet

Lived in this House

Born 1795 Died 1821

Wentworth Place as it is today

South End Green in 1819

When Lawn Bank came on the market in 1920, a
memorial fund was started towards the purchase
of the house, over half coming from America. The
Hampstead Borough Council now holds title in per-
petuity.

The Borough of Hampstead is very ancient. Along
one side of it ran Watling Street of the Roman occupation. Situated, as it is, on high ground, the view
from Well Walk, where the Spa had been in earlier
days and the Keats brothers lived in 1817-18, then
ranged from Westminster Abbey to Gravesend including the Dome of St Paul's. From the Heath today
the same spread of London can be seen. Keats House
in Keats Grove is located further down at the south
end of the Heath. The northern section of London,
known under the general name of Hampstead, is still
one of its attractive suburbs.

A. Edward Newton in *A Tourist in Spite of Himself*
has well described the interest and charm of Hampstead:

*A century ago, it was a not too remote village, much
frequented by authors, and artists in search of quiet
and fresh air. Every inch calls to mind some pleasing
memory: there once stood a famous tavern 'The
Upper Flask,' patronized by Pope and Steele and
celebrated by Richardson in* Clarissa Harlow. *To
this corner Johnson came with Goldsmith, to that
Lamb and Coleridge, Keats and Leigh Hunt. It was*

to 'Jack Straw's Castle' that Dickens invited his future biographer, John Forster, to 'come for a red-hot chop and a good glass of wine,' and it was from the tea garden of 'The Spaniards' that Mrs Bardell was unexpectedly conducted to Fleet Prison, there to meet and be released by Mr Pickwick.

When John returned to Hampstead from Bedhampton in early February, he must have been full of emotion, longing to see Fanny Brawne. He had declared his love on Christmas Day 1818 and knew it was reciprocated. The sore throat that kept him indoors at Old Mill House was still bothering him and he apparently saw few persons except the dull Reynolds sisters who were visiting the Dilkes and, of course, his secret sweetheart. In an earlier chapter, I suggested it would have been simpler if John had worn his heart on his sleeve. In spite of all his efforts at secrecy, the 'daws' did not fail to 'peck at' it during more than a hundred years, granting little credit to him and none to Fanny. Yet he did succeed in baffling his friends. Severn said, when John and he left England for Rome, that he 'was not aware of Keats being more than a common acquaintance' of Miss Brawne. Fanny herself was so bound by his wishes not to disclose their relationship that she wrote to his sister on 1st February 1821,

I know I may trust to you never to mention me either

now – or at any future time as connected with your brother – as I know he would dislike that sort of gossiping way in which people not concerned mention those things.

After John's death she again warned his sister:

I have not mentioned your brother. To no one else but you would I mention him. I will suffer no one but you to speak to me of him.

All John ever told his brother was that Miss Brawne, compared to her raw faced friend, Caroline Robinson, who was visiting her, was as 'superior as a rose to a dandelion'. Gentle Mrs Brawne, realising what was taking place did not interfere. Doubtless she encouraged her daughter to continue going out with other friends, hoping this affair with the impetuous young poet would wear off.[17] Fanny was eighteen and could not act without her mother's consent.

   Mrs Brawne had every right to be conservative about her daughter's choice of a husband. Fanny was not descended from an undistinguished family. John de Brawne, her ancestor, had come over at the Conquest and members of the Brawne family had held office under Henry VIII and the Stuarts. Her mother, born Frances Ricketts, was a lady of West Indian connections and some little fortune. Her grandfather's marriage with Jane Richardson brought the Brawne family interesting connections; one sister of her Richardson grandmother married Joseph Vernon, an accomplished actor at Drury Lane; another sister married William Brummell, private secretary of Lord North, Prime Minister to George III. His son, 'Beau Brummell,' was her father's first cousin.

That John was happy in his love and as content as his morbid but high spirited nature allowed him to be, there are many signs. After his great productive period of 1819 and his unhappy separation from Fanny that followed, then only did his resentment against fate and even against love become an obsession. From the beginning of February until the end of May he wrote practically no letters to anybody besides his sister and brother. The long journal letter to George covering his doings and thoughts from February to May showed no trace of depression or doubt, or any lack of confidence and happiness in the life he was living. In fact there was no reason for disliking it. He was seeing Fanny constantly and having his 'thousand kisses'. The journal letter to George, full of Keatsian touches, contained the contented picture he drew of himself when writing by his own fireside:

> *the fire is at its last click – I am sitting with my back to it with one foot rather askew upon the rug and the other with the heel a little elevated from the carpet – I am writing this on the Maid's tragedy which I have read since tea with Great pleasure – Besides*

this volume of Beaumont & Fletcher – there are on
the tabl[e] two volumes of chaucer and a new work
of Tom Moores call'd 'Tom Cribb's memorial to
Congress – nothing in it – these are trifles but I re-
quire nothing so much of you as that you will give
me a little description of yourselves, however it may
be when you are writing to me – Could I see the
same thing done of any great Man long since dead it
would be a great delight: As to know in what posi-
tion Shakspeare sat when he began 'To be or not to
be" – such thing[s] become interesting from dis-
tance of time or place.

Fanny Brawne and John usually walked on the
Heath when the weather was fine. Fanny, a very
level headed girl, was indignant over the way Abbey
treated John's little sister whom she had never met.
Probably her interest was responsible for the extra
attention John was now to give his sister. From February to April his letters to his sister are unusually fre-
quent. Even if he did not reveal the reason for his increased concern in the child's welfare, Fanny was the
mainspring of his attempt to interest his sister and
make her happier. Naturally too he wished to share
his own happiness with her.

. . . be careful not to let the idle and retired Life you
lead fix any awkward habit of behaviour on you –
whether you sit or walk – endeavor to let it be in a
seemely and if possible a graceful manner. . . .

In all your little troubles think of me with the
thought that there is at least one person in England
who if he could would help you out of them.

When the child was being prepared for confirmation in March she faced questions on dogma which
she sent to John. He answered all her questions, resolved her doubts, revealing intimate knowledge of
the Bible and signed himself: 'Your affectionate Parson, John'. Sometimes in his letters, to stimulate her
imagination, he would elfishly claim partiality for
something she, too, liked, such as a globe of gold fish;
he told her that 'well ventilated,'

> *they would preserve all their beautiful silver and*
> *Crimson – Then I would put it before a handsome*
> *painted window and shade it all round with myrtles*
> *and Japonicas. I should like the window to open*
> *onto the Lake of Geneva – and there I'd sit and read*
> *all day like the picture of somebody reading.*

John was able to relax his mind in mid-February and
begin his superb, calm, slow paced *Eve of St Mark.*
He told George he wrote it 'quite in the spirit of Town
quietude'. Not in the mood to finish it, however, he
produced nothing for the next two months except the
sonnet, 'Why did I laugh tonight,' which was a graph-
ic restatement of the fascination he felt for the 'high
mead' of death, expressed several times before in his
poems – *On Death,* 'When I have fears that I may

cease to be,' *To my Brothers, The Pot of Basil,* and
the 'Bright Star' sonnet.

If he suffered ups and downs in mood, he gave no
signs of unhappiness. It was characteristic of his alert
spirit when stirred that he took it upon himself to re-
prove and thrash a butcher boy for harming a kitten.
Cowden Clarke saw him a Hampstead after this encounter and thought 'he was in fine health and spirits'.
But no man could run the gamut of so many emotions
as Keats had experienced since his return from Scotland, through Tom's illness and death and falling
in love, without its having an exhausting effect. John
admitted his lassitude to George on 13th March.

> *I know not why Poetry and I have been so distant
> lately I must make some advances soon or she will
> cut me entirely.*

It is difficult to understand why the learned author
of *John Keats: The Living Year* should try to find a
reason for this period of unproductiveness by attributing it to drunkenness on the part of Keats. The only
authority he is able to cite is a generally discredited
statement written in Haydon's journal after the poet's
death. What Haydon said about Keats was a palpab-
ly false accusation of despondency over his failure as
a poet. Haydon wrote of John that:

> *Unable to bear the sneer of ignorance or the attacks*

M

of envy, not having strength of mind enough to buckle himself together like a porcupine and present nothing but prickles to his enemies, he began to despond and flew to dissipation as a relief . . . For six weeks he was scarcely sober. . . .

Mr Gittings has chosen the lurid title 'Dissipation and Darkness' for the chapter of his book covering February and March 1819, to which dates he arbitrarily allocated Keats's 'six weeks' of alleged drunkenness. His description of the effect of this period seems quite fantastic to me:

The whole pattern of these six weeks, particularly of this month of March, favours the essential truth of Haydon's account. The painter was watching the poet with alarm. Quarter-day was again coming close; Haydon's appeal became passionately urgent. 'Before the 20th if you could help me it would be nectar and manna and all the blessings of gratified thirst.' When he finally denounced Keats, it was for leading him on, 'step by step, day by day'. The way he put this monstrous accusation itself clearly shows that he had watched daily and with horror the spectacle of Keats, elusive, often in Town, doing no work, raising no money, caught in the whirlpool of some passionate crisis of his own, behaving in a way that, to the agitated and egotistical painter, could only seem 'scarcely sober'.

But the facts are quite different. The letters of

Keats, well known for their reliability and truth, are
the only accurate source, in fact the only source, of
information covering February and March 1819.
John had tried without success to raise money to lend
Haydon before leaving for Bedhampton in January.
On his return in February he wrote to his sister on
11th February and to George on 14th February that
he had to take care of himself and keep in the house.
Before 8th March, however, he had begun again to
try to raise the money Haydon wanted. On that date
he wrote to his friend:

> *You must be wondering where I am and what I am
> about! I am mostly at Hampstead ... Nor must you
> think I have forgotten you. No, I have about every
> three days been at Abbey's and the Law[y]ers. Do
> let me know how you have been getting on ... I
> have not been to see you because all my going out
> has been to town and that has been a great deal.
> Write soon.*

This letter is clear evidence that John was making
repeated attempts to help his friend. Haydon's per-
ennial need of help is shown by his reply on 10th
March:

> *My dear Keats — Now I feel the want of your your
> promised assistance — as soon as it is convenient it
> would indeed be a great, the greatest of blessings. I
> shall come and see you as soon as this contest is clear*

of my hands. I cannot before, every moment is so precious. –

There is nothing whatsoever to show that the poet and the painter were seeing one another at any time in February and March. The latter was not 'watching' Keats daily. He was otherwise occupied as his 10th March letter indicates. There is not a straw to clutch at for the theory which Mr Gittings postulates, that Haydon stood aghast and 'horrified' at the spectacle of the 'elusive,' idle and 'scarcely sober' poet.

The letters John wrote to his sister, two in February and three in March and the long journal letter to George which was begun on 14th February and kept at 'day after day' are a refutation of the 'Dissipation and Darkness' theories of Mr Gittings. One has only to read the clear and salient information contained in these letters, telling what John was doing during February and March, to be convinced of that fact.

A more sensible and probable view of the condition and state of mind of Keats between the period of inspiration which produced the two 'Eves' and his new surge in April leading to the great odes is that he was replenishing his store of creative force. In the lull between February and April he had finally gained sufficiently in knowledge and wisdom to enable him, as he put it, 'to bear all naked truths and to envisage circumstances all calm.' John wrote to George: 'I am straining after particles of light in the midst of a great darkness.' He had at last come to the conclusion that egotism and evil are inherent in human beings and must be put up with.

Egotistic poets, he supposed, might have their points too as well as a negatively capable poet, like Shakespeare, who could express the instinctive impulses, feelings, and thoughts of men or animals and who led 'a life of continual allegory.' Of course 'a man's life of any worth' would be such a life. This opinion of Keats was borne out fifty years later by Ralph Waldo Emerson, a more systematic philosopher, who wrote:

> *The moment our discourse rises above the ground line of familiar facts and is influenced by passion or exalted by thought, it clothes itself in images . . . hence good writing and brilliant discourse are perpetual allegories.*[18]

The first test that Keats had to meet in his new 'all calm' stoicism, with regard to the facts of life, was in his relationship with Fanny Brawne. On 3rd April 1819 Dilke moved to Westminster and leased his half of Wentworth Place to Mrs Brawne. For nearly three months, until John went to Shanklin with James Rice at the end of June, Fanny and he lived in adjoining houses under the same roof and in the same garden. The poems which he now composed show the uplift on his emotions, of daily intimacy with Fanny. Though so ardent a lover that he longed, as he afterwards wrote Fanny, to live 'but three summer days – three such days with you I could fill with more delight than fifty common years could ever contain,' John was too practical a man not to realise that he could not support a wife and so that marriage with Fanny was impossible.

Hence a struggle was bound to go on between passion for his love and rebellion against enslavement. He expressed this rebellion in his April ode to Fanny beginning:

> *What can I do to drive away*
> *Remembrance from my eyes? for they have seen,*
> *Aye, an hour ago, my brilliant Queen!*
> *Touch has a memory. O say, love, say,*
> *What can I do to kill it and be free*
> *In my old liberty?*

The answer in this case was – nothing!

Meantime in April, quite by chance, he met Coleridge for the first time. Coleridge had resided for years in Highgate Village and is buried there. Though Highgate, especially Millfield Lane, was one of John's favourite walks, he had never encountered Coleridge. He described to George this first interview:

> *Last Sunday I took a Walk towards highgate and in*
> *the lane that winds by the side of Lord Mansfield's*

*park I met Mr Green our Demonstrator at Guy's in
conversation with Coleridge – I joined them, after
enquiring by a look whether it would be agreeable
– I walked with him a[t] his alderman-after-dinner
pace for near two miles I suppose. In those two Miles
he broached a thousand things – let me see if I can
give you a list – Nightingales, Poetry – on Poetical
Sensation – Metaphysics – Different genera and spe-
cies of Dreams – Nightmare – a dream accompanied
by a sense of touch – single and double touch – A
dream related – First and second consciousness –
the difference explained between will and Volition
– so m[an]y metaphysicians from a want of smoking
– the second consciousness – Monsters – the Kraken
– Mermaids – Southey believes in them – Southey's
belief too much diluted – a Ghost story – Good
morning – I heard his voice as he came towards me
– I heard it as he moved away – I heard it all the
interval – if it may be called so.*

After Keats had long been dead and his fame as a
poet was beginning to be acknowledged, Coleridge
wrote, under the date of 14th August 1832, his recollection of meeting Keats:

*A loose, slack, not well-dressed youth met Mr ——
and myself in a lane near Highgate. – knew him,
and spoke. It was Keats. He was introduced to me,
and stayed a minute or so. After he had left us a little
way, he came back and said 'let me carry away the
memory, Coleridge, of having pressed your hand!'*

'There is death in that Hand', I said to —— when Keats had gone; yet this was, I believe, before the consumption showed itself distinctly.[19]

Coleridge evidently drew upon his imagination in writing of Keats in his *Table Talk*. He had written a letter, the day before he made the entry in the book, in which he used the phrase 'There was death in that dear hand' referring to the passing of a friend with whom he had often shaken hands.[20] Coleridge forgot the name of Green with whom he was walking when Keats met them, but, by association of ideas, he used the phrase of the letter, writing it in his *Table Talk* to dramatise his account of meeting the younger poet, then still active and vigorous, with whom he probably never shook hands at all.

Possibly the rambling talk of Coleridge may have spurred the mind of Keats into action. Shortly after encountering Coleridge strolling with Green, John expounded to George his serene 'Vale of Soul-making' philosophy. He called this system of soul-making the parent of all the more palpable and personal schemes of redemption. This thinking was, I believe, responsible for the humanism and calm serenity of mood in which he composed the great odes.

By the end of April John had gained complete control of himself and could express his emotions symbolically to the same effect[21] as in the personal, uncontrolled outburst he had addressed to Fanny in the ode; and he did so in his lovely ballad *La belle dame sans merci.*

Copying it in his journal letter, he wrote to George, without letting him into his secret:

> *And there I shut her wild, wild eyes*
> *With kisses four*
> *Why four Kisses – you will say – why four because*
> *I wish to restrain the headlong impetuosity of my*
> *Muse – she would have fain said 'score' without*
> *hurting the rhyme – but we must temper the Imagi-*
> *nation as the Critics say with Judgment.*

He continued his calmness and control when he composed the six great odes beginning with the *Ode to Psyche* and ending with the *Ode to Autumn.* They represent, to paraphrase his own words, his 'Top of Sovereignty'.

The *Ode to Psyche* written at the end of April voiced his love for the Greek deities. Enclosing the text of the poem in the journal letter to George he explained: 'The following Poem – the last I have written is the first and the only one with which I have taken even moderate pains. I have for the most part dash'd of[f] my lines in a hurry. This I have done leisurely – I think it reads the more richly for it and will I hope encourage me to write other thing[s] in even a more peac[e]able and healthy spirit'. The healthy spirit of stoicism he had achieved, giving him control of his personal moods and his love urge, enabled him symbolically to create those odes and render them as perfect art. The odes to *A Nightingale,* *Grecian Urn, Melancholy* and *Indolence* followed in quick succession, a truly marvellous output in a single month by a single genius.

The *Ode to a Nightingale* is more poignant, melodious and personal than the others. It seems also more romantic from the knowledge we have of the manner of its composition. It is not difficult to visualise Keats sitting there under a plum tree, as Sir Sydney Colvin suggests, in the garden of Wentworth Place enraptured into song himself by memories of songs of nightingales. The ode tells how impossible it was for him to escape from painful realities of life into an ideal world of natural beauty.

To my mind, however, the *Ode on a Grecian Urn* takes precedence over all others because of its restraint, its beauty of imagery, its universal quality and its look toward eternity. 'More endeared, it pipes to the spirit ditties of no tone.' The sylvan historian of the urn is speaking. Love is always warm and still to be enjoyed and always will be. Human passion does leave us cloyed. The superiority of art as expressed in the 'Urn' represents never fading beauty and an eternal truth. The men and women of the urn cannot fade. They are constant and lie outside time. They 'tease us out of thought as doth eternity'.

The final message of the Urn:

> *Beauty is truth, truth beauty that is all*
> *Ye know on earth and all ye need to know.*

has raised the eyebrows of some critics. But subtle
Emily Dickinson grasped the idea of Keats when she
wrote from her Amherst retreat:

> *I died for beauty, but was scarce*
> *Adjusted in the tomb,*
> *When one who died for truth was lain*
> *In an adjoining room.*
>
> *He questioned softly why I failed?*
> *'For beauty,' I replied.*
> *'And I for truth — the two are one*
> *We brethren are,' he said.*[22]

There are different sorts of truth such as theological
truths and scientific truths; hence there is no single
concept of truth. Its precise meaning must vary according to the field of thought. In the mind of Keats
this field was 'the mighty abstract Idea I have of
Beauty in all things'. There is a 'Real of Beauty,' he
once wrote. He had reiterated this thought often
enough. 'I never can feel certain of any truth but
from a clear perception of its Beauty' and again, 'the
excellence of every Art is its intensity, capable of
making all disagreeables evaporate from their being

in close relationship with Beauty and Truth' – . He
told George that Lord Byron 'describes what he sees
– I describe what I imagine. Mine is the hardest task.
You see the immense difference'.

In *The Romantic Imagination*, Sir Cecil M. Bowra
has explained how it works:

'The belief that "beauty is truth, truth beauty" is
true for the artist while he is concerned with his art.
It is no less true that, while he is at work, this is all
that he knows for certain and all that he needs to
know for the proper pursuit of his special task. Un-
less he believes this, he is in danger of ruining his art.
The *Ode on the Grecian Urn* tells what great art
means to those who create it, and so long as this doc-
trine is not applied beyond its proper confines, it is
not only clear but true.'

CHAPTER ELEVEN

SHANKLIN AND WINCHESTER:
A SEASON OF MISTS: 1819

ALTHOUGH at the end of May Keats had just completed his great burst of inspiration, it brought him no peace of mind. He felt the need still to 'feed his growing heart'.[23] Hard up and in doubt what to do, he consulted Marianne Jeffrey of Teignmouth:

I want you to do me a Favour; which I will first ask and then tell you the reasons. Enquire in the Villages round Teignmouth if there is any Lodging commodious for its cheapness; and let me know where it is and what price. I have the choice as it were of two Poisons (yet I ought not to call this a Poison) the one is voyaging to and from India for a few years; the other is leading a fevrous life alone with Poetry – This latter will suit me best; for I cannot resolve to give up my Studies. . . . I have been always till now almost as careless of the world as a fly – my troubles were all of the Imagination – My Brother George always stood between me and any dealings with the world. Now I find I must buffet it – I must take my stand upon some vantage ground and begin to fight – I must choose between despair & energy – I choose the latter – though the world has taken on a quakerish look with me, which I once thought was impossible –

Miss Jeffrey advised against the Indiaman with which advice John concurred but he corrected her reasoning: 'Your advice about the Indiaman is a very wise advice, because it justs suits me, though you are a little in the wrong concerning its destroying the energies of the Mind: on the contrary it would be the finest thing in the world to strengthen them – To be thrown among people who care not for you, with whom you have no sympathies forces the Mind upon its own resources, and leaves it free to make its speculations of the differences of human character and to class them with the calmness of a Botanist. An Indiaman is a little world'.

On asking Abbey for money he received a new blow. His aunt, the widow of his mother's brother, Captain Midgely John Jennings, whose participation in the naval battle of Camperdown he had proudly boasted of at school, was about to bring a suit in Chancery to break the trust set up by his grandfather John Jennings. Abbey told him this suit would tie up payments from the Estate. He had been counting on his share of Tom's money. Too generous and open handed for his own good, John had lent considerable sums to his friends. His request for payment of these loans brought no favourable replies except from Haslam who owed George a small sum. Brown, however, came to the rescue with an idea. He offered to supply a plot for a tragedy to be called *Otho the Great*, the text of which in blank verse Keats would write. Brown planned to let his half of Wentworth Place as usual for the summer, to take a short walking trip, then join John later in the country and help him. Meantime he would supply living expenses. The eyes of these two were 'bright' with the 'purpose' of having Kean act in *Otho the Great;* he would surely bring in money for them both.

James Rice and he agreed to spend a month together in the country, going on 27th June 1819 at Rice's suggestion to Shanklin on the Isle of Wight instead of to Bradley in Devonshire which Marianne Jeffrey had recommended. When John first saw Shanklin in 1817 he had written Reynolds an enthusiastic description of it:

> *Shanklin is a most beautiful place – sloping wood and meadow ground reaches round the Chine, which is a cleft between the Cliffs of the depth of nearly 300 feet at least. This cleft is filled with trees & bushes in the narrow parts; and as it widens becomes bare, if it were not for primroses on one side, which spread to the very verge of the Sea, and some fishermen's huts on the other, perched midway in the Ballustrades of beautiful green Hedges along their steps down to the sands.*

He should have been happy in so delightful a site by the sea he loved, but disease was beginning to spread

its pall over him. Rice was ill, too. Their natural affection did not prevent their having a depressing effect
upon each other. July turned out to be a distressing
month. John wrote to Dilke on 31st July that Rice had
tried to wash away their melancholy with puns. He
added: 'Rice and I passed rather a dull time of it. I
confess I cannot bear a sick person in a House especially alone – it weighs on me day and night.'

At the end of July, Charles Brown, that robust way-
farer, turned up from his travels, much to John's relief. They set to work at once on the composition of
Otho the Great. Having proved to himself that he
could write romantic poetry, Keats longed to try his
hand at truly dramatic verse. He had been studying
Shakespeare's plays in detail since 1817. A dramatic
tragedy now offered an opportunity not only to make
much needed money but to put him on the way towards his real ambition in prosody. He believed he
could restore naturalism to the writing of plays. 'One
of my Ambitions,' he said, 'is to make as great a revo-
lution in modern dramatic writing as Kean has done
in acting.' In commenting later on the *Eve of St
Agnes* to Taylor he wrote: 'Two or three such Poems,
if God should spare me, written in the course of the
next six years, would be a famous gradus ad Parnas-
sum altissimum. I mean they would nerve me up to
the writing of a few fine Plays – my greatest ambition
– when I do feel ambitious'.

A prodigious amount of work was done by Keats at Shanklin and Winchester during the summer and autumn of 1819. Modestly he made light of his co-operation in *Otho the Great* – 'Brown likes the Tragedy very much,' he wrote to Taylor on 5th September, 'but he is not a fit judge as I have only acted as Midwife to his plot and of course he will be fond of his child'. But Brown told the true story in his *Life of John Keats*:

> *At Shanklin he undertook a difficult task; I engaged to furnish him with the title, characters, and dramatic conduct of a tragedy, and he was to enwrap it in poetry. The progress of this work was curious, for while I sat opposite to him, he caught my description of each scene entire, with the characters to be brought forward, the events, and everything connected with it. This he went on, scene after scene, never knowing or inquiring into the scene which was to follow, until four acts were completed. It was then he required to know at once all the events that were to occupy the fifth act; I explained them to him, but after patient hearing and some thought, he insisted that many incidents in it were too humorous, or, as he termed them, too melodramatic. He wrote the fifth act in accordance with his own views, and so contented was I with his poetry that at the time, and for a long time after, I thought he was in the right.*

Excellence of writing is usually based on the experi-
N

ences, real or imaginary, of the writer. Keats made
no exception to this rule in endowing Ludolph, the
lover in *Otho the Great,* with the torments of jealousy
and love pangs he himself was suffering. The tragedy
of the tragedy proved to be that Kean went on tour
to America, unexpectedly to the authors. *Otho the
Great* never was produced until 1950, then only twice.

In mid-August Brown and Keats decided to move
to Winchester in hope of finding a reference library.
Keats finished the last act of *Otho* at Winchester by
himself, as Brown said, and also his narrative poem
of the snake woman *Lamia* which he had begun at
Shanklin. He also worked over and smoothed out
The Eve of St Agnes, improved the 'Bright Star' sonnet and revised from a previous composition *The
Fall of Hyperion, A Dream.*

Winchester was a welcome relief after Shanklin.
He had exchanged, he told Fanny Brawne, 'a little
coffin of a room'. . .'for a large one where I can promenade at my pleasure – looks out on to a beautiful
— blank side of a house. It is strange I should like it
better than the view of the sea from our window at
Shanklin'. He gave his sister on 28th August a description of the venerable city of Winchester:

> it is the pleasantest *Town* I ever was in, and has the
> most reccommendations of any. There is a fine
> Cathedrall which to me is always a source of amuse-

*ment, part of it built 1400 years ago; and the more
modern by a magnificent Man, you may have read
of in our History, called William of Wickham. The
whole town is beautifully wooded – From the Hill
at the eastern extremity you see a prospect of Streets,
and old Buildings mixed up with Trees. Then there
are the most beautiful streams about I ever saw –
full of Trout. There is the Foundation of St Croix
about half a mile in the fields – a charity greatly
abused. We have a Collegiate School, a roman catho-
lic School, a chapel ditto and a Nunnery! And what
improves it all is, the fashionable inhabitants are all
gone to Southampton. . . . I have still been hard at
work, having completed a Tragedy I think I spoke
of to you. But there I fear all my labour will be
thrown away for the present, as I hear Mr Kean is
going to America. For all I can guess I shall remain
here till the middle of October – when Mr Brown
will return to his house at Hampstead: whither I
shall return with him.*

Where did Keats live in Winchester? Perhaps he
nearly identified his location as just off High Street in
his letter to Reynolds of 21st September:

*The first night tho' of our arrival here there was a
slight uproar took place at about 10 o' the clock. We
heard distinctly a noise patting down the high Street
as of a walking cane of the good old Dowager breed;
and a little minute after we heard a less voice ob-
serve "What a noise the ferril made – it must be*

loose" – Brown wanted to call the Constables but I
observed twas only a little breeze and would soon
pass over.

A lane from High Street is the direct approach to
the path under the ancient lime trees leading to the
front of the Cathedral, that John said he generally
took. 'On the other side of the building,'(the Cathedral) he told George, 'I pass through one of the old
city gates and then you are in one College Street
through which I pass and at the end thereof crossing
some meadows and at last a country alley of gardens
I arrive, that is, my worship arrives at the foundation
of Saint Cross, which is a very interesting old place,
. . . Then I pass across St Cross meadows till you come
to the most beautifully clear river.' It was in these
meadows that the *Ode to Autumn* was inspired if not
composed. Keats's walk led past the house on College
Street in which Jane Austen had died but two years
before.

Keats had told Fanny Brawne that he would not
return to London if his fate did not 'turn up Pam or
at least a Court-card' but, as his letters to her from
Shanklin show, he found the anguish of being away
more painful than the emotional and nervous strain
of being near her. The combination of being a jealous, possessive lover, intensely desiring his loved one,
of being conscious that he had no money with which

to support her and of having a progressive disease
that was gaining on him, was devastating.

The letters of John to Fanny Brawne in the summer of 1819 fall, I think, into two groups. His first
letters are normal and lover-like; the second group
belong to his reaction to a realisation of his physical
decadence and doubtful future. No wonder Fanny
told him that she 'must not have any more such letters' as this:

> I have two luxuries to brood over in my walks, your
> Loveliness and the hour of my death. O that I could
> have possession of them both in the same minute. I
> hate the world: it batters too much the wings of my
> self-will, and would I could take a sweet poison from
> your lips to send me out of it.

Perhaps John had begun this summer actually to
detect traces of blood in his saliva. Putting a handker-
chief to his mouth he would be aware of it. In his
frank letter to Reynolds, written from Winchester, in
which he questioned the soundness of his heart and
lungs, Keats said:

> I feel my body too weak to support me to the height,
> I am obliged continually to check myself and [strive
> to] be nothing. It would be vain for me to endeavour
> after a more reasonable manner of writing to you. I
> have nothing to speak of but myself – and what can
> I say but what I feel? If you should have any reason

*to regret this state of excitement in me, I will turn
the tide of your feelings in the right Channel, by
mentioning that it is the only state for the best sort
of Poetry – that is all I care for, all I live for.*[24]

Very probably incipient tubercular germs had been
at work in John's body since the stay at Teignmouth
and now, with his medical knowledge, he had become aware of them.

It was a period of extreme and troublesome doubt.
He wrote to Taylor from Winchester: 'I equally dislike the favour of the public with the love of a woman
– they are both cloying treacle to the wings of inde-
pendence'. But sometimes in a hopeful mood he
would speak to Fanny of their honeymoon: 'We might
spend a pleasant year at Berne or Zurich – if it should
please Venus to hear my 'Beseech thee to hear us O
Goddess'. Even then he added defiantly: 'And if she
should hear god forbid we should be what people
call, *settle* . . . Better be imprudent moveables than
prudent fixtures'.

This summer of 1819 surely brought with it defiance on the part of Keats who bullied not only Fanny
but his publishers as well. Brown, on whom he was
then depending for financial aid, told Keats, not too
truthfully, that he ought to be alone at Winchester
without any interruption for the month of September
in order to compose and that he, Brown, was going

to visit John Snook at Bedhampton. On 24th August in order to provide funds for Keats, he offered to guarantee Taylor the payment of a loan to be made to Keats. Taylor was on holiday but Woodhouse came to the rescue with an advance of £50, part of which he told Hessey to hold back. Hessey sent Keats £30 on 5th September and Brown went away. Meantime John had ceased writing to Fanny and also failed to go and see her at Hampstead when he went to London on 11th September. This unexpected London visit was the result of another blow to the Keats family. It had fallen this time on George, desperately in need of money. He put all the money he had into a boat carrying freight along the Ohio river. The boat sank. He wrote asking John to go to Abbey on his behalf.

On arriving in London Keats saw Woodhouse and Hessey. He was most wayward and cynical in his attitude. He wanted some of his recent poetry published in order to get money. Hessey told him this was impossible. He had been revising *The Eve of St Agnes* and insisted he should make all too plain the carnal relations between Porphyro and Madeline. He added he didn't write poems for women to read. He talked in the same way about his snake woman Lamia. Taylor, when he heard of Keats's attitude, went so far as to write to Woodhouse that he would not publish any new Keats volume on any such basis. This threat John never knew. The tact and patience of

Woodhouse caused him to give up his defiance. When the 1820 volume was published *The Eve of St Agnes* resumed its magical beauty and *Lamia* retained its original appeal.

Woodhouse wrote to Keats that he was likely to see Reynolds at Bath where both were to be on vacation. Confident they would discuss his proposal to put spice into Porphyro's romance, John asked Reynolds for his opinion:

> *Tonight I am all in a mist; I scarcely know what's what. . . . I shall beg leave to have a third opinion in the first discussion you have with Woodhouse – just half-way – between both. You know I will not give up my argument – In my walk today I stoop'd under a rail way that lay across my path, and ask'd myself "Why I did not get over" Because, answered I, "no one wanted to force you under –" I would give a guinea to be a reasonable man – good sound sense – a says what he thinks, and does what he says man – and did not take snuff. They say men near death however mad they may have been, come to their senses – I hope I shall here in this letter –*

The first part of this letter sounds like the naughty lad he had become; the last part like the reasonable man he longed to be.

Upon his return to Winchester on 15th September, the peace and calm of the cathedral city brought a serenity of spirit to Keats. Brown had gone and he

was alone. On the following Sunday, 19th September
– a memorable day in his career – he walked through
the fields towards the St Cross Hospice. Writing to
Reynolds two days later he described his sensations:
'How beautiful the season is now – How fine the air. A
temperate sharpness about it. Really, without joking,
chaste weather – Dian skies – I never lik'd stubble-
fields so much as now – Aye better than the chilly
green of Spring. Somehow a stubble-plain looks
warm – in the same way that some pictures look
warm – This struck me so much in my Sunday's walk
that I composed upon it'. The poem he wrote on his
return from his walk was the sensuous, imaginative
and beautiful *Ode to Autumn*.

A mood of marvellous quietness freed his genius
to express these perfect stanzas of song. Shrugging
off his failure to obtain any immediate help for George
he had penned George a cheerful, carefree message
the day before he composed the *Ode to Autumn*.

*We are certainly in a very low estate: I say we, for I
am in such a situation that were it not for the assistance of Brown & Taylor I must be as badly off as a
Man can be. I could not raise any sum by the promise of any Poem – no, not by the mortgage of my
intellect. We must wait a little while. I really have
hopes of success. I have finish'd a Tragedy which if
it succeeds will enable me to sell what I may have in
Manuscript to a good a[d]vantage. I have pass'd my*

time in reading, writing and fretting – the last I in-
tend to give up and stick to the other two. They are
the only chances of benefit to us. . . . With my incon-
stant disposition it is no wonder that this morning,
amid all our bad times and misfortunes, I should
feel so alert and well spirited. At this moment you
are perhaps in a very different state of Mind. It is
because my hopes are very paramount to my des-
pair. I have been reading over a part of a short poem
I have composed lately call'd 'Lamia' – and I am
certain there is that sort of fire in it which must take
hold of people in some way – give them either plea-
sant or unpleasant sensation. What they want is a
sensation of some sort. I wish I could pitch the Key
of your spirits as high as mine is – but your organ loft
is beyond the reach of my voice.

The calmness of autumn that had come to Keats
showed itself in the conduct of his personal affairs.
He usually relied on Brown for advice in practical
matters but Charles had been away from him since
early September. On his own initiative he decided it
would be best not to return to Hampstead for the
winter. He would instead settle in London and write
for the press. He thought he could support himself
by writing critical reviews of books and plays. He
would not have to depend on his friend or see Fanny
next door.

Brown returned late in September to Bedhampton,
where he was supposed to be staying, from Ireland or

wherever he actually had been, to find four letters from Keats awaiting him. The bald fact about Brown's visit to Ireland or London is that he went for the purpose of consummating an intimacy with his housemaid, Abigail Donahue, under a pretext of marriage that satisfied her. Keats was not aware of the alleged marriage and Brown, knowing John's ethical code about the responsibilities of marriage, concealed the trip from him. Brown was thick skinned and selfish in what he did. He wanted a son, who would inherit his brains and the brawn of Abigail, without the incumbrance of a wife.

After Brown read the letters from Winchester he hurried over to see Keats. He approved the idea of writing for the press and disapproved living alone in London. Knowing Keats, he was right in thinking John couldn't stand being alone. However it was agreed between them that Dilke, who now had a house in Westminster, should find lodgings for John nearby. A week later, 8th October 1819, they returned to London. On Sunday, 10th October, John went for the day to visit Brown at Hampstead. He saw Fanny. There had been more than three months of separation, two of them enforced repression on his part. The reunion proved a happy one for Keats. His love burst into flames again.

When he returned that evening to his lodging overlooking the gardens of Westminster Abbey, he poured out his love in a letter. His sonnet which he sent with it was symptomatic of the decline in his health, his prospects and his happiness. It was the sad symbol of what really was happening — a fading away of all the sweets of life:

> *Faded the flower and all its budded charms*
> *Faded the sight of beauty from my eyes*
> *Faded the shape of beauty from my arms*
> *Faded the voice, warmth, whiteness, paradise —*
> *Vanished unseasonably . . .*

CHAPTER TWELVE

THE WORLD'S SLOW STAIN: 1820

WHEN KEATS arrived at 25 College Street, Westminster, Dilke noticed the change in him. 'His mind was all in a ferment.' But after he saw Fanny on Sunday he gave up all thought of rebelling against his love as he had in the spring and summer. Fearful that everything was 'fading,' he surrendered unconditionally to his emotions. His disease was destroying his control and increasing his longing. Though he was morbidly jealous of Fanny he never showed, so long as he lived, any further rebellion against his enslavement.

Brown may have been callous and mercenary in his own amorous instincts but he had the decency to be sympathetic in a genuine attack of love. John had set himself the task of copying his poem's 'out fair' with a view to publication. Nevertheless when Mrs Brawne invited him to spend a few days at Wentworth Place, he dropped his work and followed his heart to Hampstead. Seeing Fanny constantly, sharing meals, watching her flit about, he was only too eager to accept Brown's suggestion that he return to Wentworth Place on his old footing. Once again settled in his own room, more or less at peace with himself, he resumed the revision of *Hyperion* and, at Brown's suggestion, started a drama, the scene of which was to be laid in the reign of King Stephen.

Notwithstanding Keats was mentally at his peak, disease made continuous work of serious composition difficult for him. He was only able to do two hundred lines in all of his tragedy called *King Stephen*. These lines show that, given time, he might have developed into a true dramatist, as Shakespeare had done, upon gaining the experience of forty years. He had the gift, apparent in his narrative poems and in this fragment, of making his characters come alive. Of the victor in battle in *King Stephen* John wrote this felicitous phrase: –

'How like a comet he goes streaming on' and described the scene after the victory in a truly Elizabethan passage:

> *Now may we lift our bruised visors up,*
> *And take the flattering freshness of the air,*
> *While the wide din of battle dies away*
> *Into times past, yet to be echoed sure*
> *In the silent pages of our chroniclers.*

He derived the facts of *King Stephen* from Holinshed's *Chronicles of England, Scotland and Ireland,* the source from which Shakespeare had adopted the facts that appear in his historical plays and tragedies.

In the latter part of October Keats attended the 'Lectures on the Dramatic Literature of the Age of Elizabeth' which Hazlitt delivered at the Surrey Institution. They covered the subjects in which he was then interested. Continuing to read Holinshed, he thought he might be able to compose a dramatic romance in the form of a narrative poem based on the love affair of the Earl of Leicester and Queen Elizabeth. There is no evidence he composed a single verse of this romance. Brown, Severn and Dilke had all noticed the sudden decline in John's health. Brown was plainly worried at his inertia. It was clear he lacked the vitality to do the hard work of composition on a serious poem he had once done. Talking together one day, their conversation turned on the idea of a comic faery poem in the Spenser stanza. 'I was glad to encourage it,' wrote Brown, 'he had not composed many stanzas before he proceeded in it with spirit. It was to be published under the feigned authorship of Lucy Vaughan Lloyd and to bear the title *The Cap and Bells*, or, which he preferred, *The Jealousies*. This occupied his mornings pleasantly. He wrote it with the greatest facility.'

The Cap and Bells was written as a parody on *Don Juan*, which Keats called 'Lord Byron's last flash poem'. He imitated the style and satirised Byron himself. The incidents in it correspond to incidents in the career of the dissolute Prince Regent, afterwards George IV. Keats worked spasmodically on it until he was finally laid low by the haemorrhage of 3rd February 1820. He left it unfinished. The unfinished stanza contains the last words of poetry he ever wrote. An interesting feature of the manuscript is his insertion between the fifty-first and fifty-second stanzas of a spontaneous emotional appeal, probably written with Fanny in mind, that had no connection at all with the story of *The Cap and Bells*.

> *This living hand, now warm and capable*
> *Of earnest grasping, would, if it were cold*
> *And in the icy silence of the tomb,*
> *So haunt thy days and chill thy dreaming nights*
> *That thou wouldst wish thine own heart dry of blood*
> *So in my veins red life might stream again,*
> *And thou be conscience-calm'd – see here it is –*
> *I hold it towards you.*

As great poetry from a great poet this final poem does not amount to much. The flight of Crafticant and the Princess in *The Cap and Bells* is, however, an example of Keats's powerful intuition. What he instinctively wrote in 1820, might be the account of an aeroplane flight today over Asia near the border of the Soviets. It has a familiar sound – the fog that delayed the start; the fliers saw the moon come up and met the rising sun; a hostile 'griffin,' buzzing about, caused panic to passengers before it sheered off; at the end they looked down on cheering crowds waving holiday flags as they arrived.

This remarkable passage in the poem, anticipating

present day travel by air, has never been commented
on, so far as I know. Crafticant tells the story with
split second, modern technique :

> *'Twas twelve o'clock at night, the weather fine,*
> *Latitude thirty-six; our scouts descry*
> *A flight of starlings making rapidly*
> *Towards Thibet. Mem.: – birds fly in the night;*
> *From twelve to half-past – wings not fit to fly*
> *For a thick fog – the Princess sulky quite*
> *Call'd for an extra shawl, and gave her nurse a bite....*
>
> *From two till half-past, dusky way we made,*
> *Above the plains of Gobi,-desert, bleak;*
> *Beheld afar off, in the hooded shade*
> *Of darkness, a great mountain (strange to speak),*
> *Spitting, from forth its sulphur-baken peak,*
> *A fan-shaped burst of blood-red, arrowy fire,*
> *Turban'd with smoke, which still away did reek,*
> *Solid with black from that eternal pyre,*
> *Upon the laden winds that scantly could respire. ....*
>
> *Five minutes thirteen seconds after three,*
> *Far in the west a mighty fire broke out,*
> *Conjectur'd, on the instant, it might be*
> *The city of Balk – 'twas Balk beyond all doubt:*
> *A griffin, wheeling here and there about,*
> *Kept reconnoitring us – doubled our guard –*
> *Lighted our torches, and kept up a shout,*
> *Till he sheer'd off – The Princess very scared –*
> *And many on their marrow-bones for death prepar'd.*

o

At half-past three arose the cheerful moon —
Bivouack'd for four minutes on a cloud . . .
About this time — making delightful way, —
Shed a quill-feather from my larboard wing . . .
At five the golden light began to spring,
With fiery shudder through the bloomed east;
At six we heard Panthea's churches ring —
The city all her unhiv'd swarms had cast,
To watch our grand approach, and hail us as we
*   pass'd. . . .*

Onward we floated o'er the panting streets,
That seem'd throughout with upheld faces paved;
Look where we will, our bird's-eye vision meets
Legions of holiday; bright standards waved,
And fluttering ensigns emulously craved
One minute's glance; a busy thunderous roar,
From square to square, among the buildings raved,
As when the sea, at flow, gluts up once more
The craggy hollowness of a wild-reefed shore.

At the turn of the year George came to England.
The purpose of his visit was to raise money for himself.
Though John was present at some festivities given
for his brother he was too unwell to accompany
George on all visits as he used to do. He contented
himself by writing to 'little George' in America trying
to amuse and cheer her in her husband's absence:

We smoke George about his little Girl, he runs the

*common beaten road of every father, as I dare say
you do of every Mother – there is no Child like his
Child – so original! original forsooth. However I
take you at your words; I have a lively faith that
yours is the very gem of all Children. Aint I its Unkle?*

This long letter dwelt with the whole period of
George's visit from 13th to 28th January. And to Mrs
Wylie, Georgiana's mother, who was disturbed over
the reason for George's visit, he made this sensible
comment: 'If George succeeds it will be better certainly that they should stop in America; if not why
not return . . . I have great hopes so far as I can judge
from what I heard from George. He should by this
time be taught alertness and prudence'.

George was never to see his brother again. He took
back with him £700. In part it was John's money. Perhaps George was unfair in accepting the loan from
him. He told Fanny Brawne: 'George ought not to
have done this – but I suppose having a family to provide for makes a man selfish'. We also know of this
loan from Abbey's letter to John dated 23rd August
1820, in reply to a request for aid in financing the
journey to Italy: 'You know that it was very much
against my will,' wrote Abbey, 'that you lent your
money to George'. Abbey asserted that bad debts had
cut down his profits and said therefore it was not
in his power to lend John anything; he capped his

refusal with an insulting postscript: 'When you are
able to call I shall be glad to see you as I should not
like to see you want "maintenance for the day" '.
What a man!

In less than a week after his brother's departure
John was stricken. On 3rd February 1820 he went to
London and returned at night on the top of the coach
without a greatcoat. Chilled through, he arrived
home at eleven o'clock flushed and nervous with a
high fever. Brown put him to bed. Blood came up in
his mouth half suffocating him. It was arterial blood.
A doctor was called and bled him. He lay awake
thinking of Fanny Brawne. Next day, 4th February,
he wrote her a note:

> *They say I must remain confined to this room for*
> *some time. The consciousness that you love me will*
> *make a pleasant prison of the house next to yours.*
> *You must come and see me frequently: this evening,*
> *without fail . . . you must see me tonight and let me*
> *hear you promise to come tomorrow.*

He sent messages also to his sister intimating it
would be a long time before he could walk the six
miles necessary to see her. He remembered how he
used to call it 'cutting across the fields'. His friends
had been most kind, he told her: 'I have so many pre-
sents of jams and jellies that they would reach side by
side the length of the sideboard'. He described the

sofa bed he now slept in downstairs and all the persons and things he could see from the window. No doubt he hoped secretly to be able to tell his sister in his next letter that Carlo, Mrs Brawne's dog, and Lappy, the pet dog of the two prim maiden ladies whom he described, had had a fight.

The weather was not kind. Spring came slowly. He could not go out and was extremely nervous. The diet of 'pseudo-victuals' allowed patients in those days and the constant blood letting had affected his heart. 'From this period,' wrote Dilke, 'his weakness & his long suffering, mental and bodily, increased – his whole mind & heart were in a whirl of contending passions – he saw nothing calmly or dispassionately'. While the health of Keats evidently grew worse as time went on, his state of mind, seems to have remained more normal than Dilke's statement would admit.

One notable result of John's serious haemorrhage was its effect on Fanny Brawne. She gave up going out or to town and made herself available to him whenever he was able to see her. John was decent enough to recognise her devotion, telling her later: 'Let me not longer detain you from going to Town – there may be no end to this imprisoning of you'. Fanny did not go. In March he asked her: 'How can you bear so long an imprisonment at Hampstead? I shall always remember it with all the gusto that a monopolizing carle should. I could build an Altar to you for it'. Without doubt Fanny had matured in the year and a half since she met the man who loved her so much. Her anxiety about him is reflected in John's notes assuring her of his progress towards health.

Although young, gay and sociable, she was also intelligent, quick at repartee, like John fond of music, and spoke French fluently. Whatever complaints John may have felt because of her other interests apart from him, he could, in truth, have none after his February attack. He was henceforth the sole object of her love and attention. Everything known of Fanny Brawne suggests that she was a woman of spirit. She could never have submitted to John Keats or tolerated his attitude, if she had not really loved him. That he appreciated it, notwithstanding his quavering moments, is shown by repeated declaration from his sick bed:

> *Thank God that you are fair and can love me without being Letter-written and sentimentaliz'd into it.*

and

> *how much more deeply then must I feel for you knowing you love me. My Mind has been the most discontented and restless one that ever was put into a body too small for it.*

But as he became convalescent with the end of spring and Fanny resumed contact with the world outside, his jealousy returned. He started to complain again. Probably it was then that he wrote the demanding ode addressed to Fanny beginning:

Physician Nature! Let my Spirit blood!

In spite of its being usually dated February 1819, there seem to be reasons for ascribing it to the summer of 1820. He was, in February 1819, not on sufficiently firm ground with Fanny to risk such a demanding code. His wings had not then been clipped and he could not safely have adopted the emphatic tone of the ode which belongs, as Edmund Blunden has noted, 'only to the private history of a dying man in love'.[25]

Comments by various writers have been made on Fanny Brawne such as, 'with her limited capacity,' she was 'too small a vessel for the love that approached that day in Dilke's room,' or 'to answer the demands which a man of Keats's temperament could not but make, called for something of a heroic quality which Fanny did not possess'.[26] How does anyone know she lacked the heroic quality to meet his demands? He did not write to her in the simple language he used in writing to his young sister. She proved her acumen, sound sense and strength of character in not resenting and destroying his bitter, insulting letters, as a flighty woman might. There is no suggestion from any source that Fanny did not understand both John and his letters. Her correspondence with Fanny Keats shows her tact, judgment and reliability.

Life for Keats had nothing left from now on except his love for Fanny Brawne. He struggled, however, to go about as he had been used to do. He was able late in March to go to the private view of Haydon's *Christ's Entry into Jerusalem*. Hazlitt and he sat in a corner witnessing Haydon's triumph. It must have been gratifying to Keats to read in *The Morning Post* of 30th March that among 'the principal persons, distinguished for rank and talent, in the company, were Sir Walter Scott, Charles Lamb, Keats and Procter'.

Brown was now thinking about his summer plans. He wanted to let his house again and be off on the road. He had been a faithful nurse to Keats since 3rd February and had borne all the expense. The rent from the house would enable him to meet it and to have his holiday. Keats on his part thought he might be happy near Hunt in Kentish Town, then one of the pretty villages surrounding London. Hunt's house was at 13 Mortimer Terrace and John was able to find a room just round the corner at 2 Weslayan Place, both of which houses are still extant in a shabby neighbourhood. In 1820, Mortimer Terrace faced open country with a fine clear view towards Hamp-

stead. Meantime Brown was preparing for his walking tour. John accompanied him as far as Gravesend,
half thinking of going in the smack, too, for the trip.
But Keats was far from well and Brown sailed alone
on 7th May 1820. They never saw each other again.

Two things had troubled John at Wentworth Place.
One was the strain of being near Fanny but not near
enough: the other concerned the presence in Brown's
household of Abigail Donohue. That Keats knew
something of what was going on we suspect, indeed
we know. In his final letter to Fanny Brawne in August 1820 possibly referring to the Brown menage, he
said: 'wherever I may be next winter – in Italy or nowhere – Brown will be living near you with his in-
decencies.' And Brown, writing to Keats in Rome in
December sought to reassure him on this matter by
saying: 'O, – I must tell you Abby is living with me
again, but not in the same capacity, – she keeps to
her own bed, & I keep myself continent'.

Now free from the nervousness and restraint which
had obsessed him at Hampstead and no longer on a
low diet, Keats was able to go for a time into company. He saw much of Hunt. He spent an evening at
Monkhouse's with Lamb and Wordsworth. He was
also invited to sup with Southey, Lamb, Wordsworth
and Haydon but was not well enough to go. He went
to the Surrey Institution to see a collection of English
portraits and laughed in his letter to Brown over the

portrait of James I 'whose appearance would disgrace
a "Society for the Suppression of Women" '. Receiv-
ing an urgent summons from his sister to come to
Walthamstow he tried to go by coach. He began to
spit blood and returned to his house. Feeling better
that same evening he called at Leigh Hunt's. Mrs
Gisborne, the friend of Shelley, was there. She recorded in her diary that a quiet pale young man, the
author of *Endymion,* came to tea and spoke in such a
low voice he could hardly be heard. When Keats re-
returned to his room he had another attack. He was
in no condition to remain in lodgings with no one to
care for him and generous Hunt took him to his own
crowded home.

The thought of Fanny haunted him. He had dreams
of her dressed as a sheperdess going to dances in the
assembly room at Well Walk. He wrote her terrible
letters telling her: 'You must be mine to die upon the
rack if I want you'. He had a delusion that prying eyes
would see their correspondence. He had been relatively independent in 1819—at least enough to mar-
vel at his infatuation. Writing then from Shanklin he
had said: 'I am indeed astonish'd to find myself so
careless of all cha[r]ms but yours—rememb[e]ring
as I do the time when even a bit of ribband was a
matter of interest with me'. No doubt he meant to be
reasonable and considerate. Although his passion for
Fanny never reached a noble level of unselfishness on

his part, it was not 'grotesque and humiliating' as some critics called it before the depth of Fanny's affection became known after her letters to Fanny Keats were published in 1938. At the time he penned his uncontrolled letters, his condition must have made him desperate. He believed he was about to begin what he called a 'posthumous existence'.

Hunt's house in Mortimer Terrace, though noisy and full of children, seemed home to him and better than solitude. In her diary Mrs Gisborne, who saw him there again on 12th July, wrote that she was 'much pained by the sight of poor Keats under sentence of death from Dr Lamb. He never spoke and looked emaciated'. Mary Novello Clarke, who had remembered him listening to music at her father's house, wrote in her *Life* of the indelible impression she retained of seeing him for the last time, half reclining on some chairs that formed a couch for him when he was staying at Leigh Hunt's house, just before leaving England for Italy, 'in which position Mrs Hunt cut his silhouette' now at Keats House.

On 10th August an event occurred that was dreadful to the disturbed mind of Keats. A letter from Fanny, his secret love, came to him with its seal broken. Outraged, he left Mortimer Terrace to go to Hampstead to tell her what had happened, intending to stay with his old friend and landlady Mrs Bentley in Well Walk. Mrs Brawne, seeing his condition, refused to let him leave her house. She and Fanny would care for him until the trip to Italy, ordered by his doctor, could be arranged. And so it came about that John was able to spend his happiest month in more than two years at the home of his betrothed.

In the first week of July the now famous 1820 volume entitled *Lamia, Isabella, The Eve of St Agnes and other Poems* had been published, price seven shillings and six pence. Keats was too ill to take any part in the event. He authorised his publishers to bring out the edition in such form as they thought best. The book had excellent reviews and probably would have sold well except for the gremlin which was for ever meddling in the affairs of the Keats family. George III died in January 1820 and the Prince Regent succeeded him as George IV. A bill was at once introduced into Parliament on his behalf to enable him to get rid of his wife Princess Caroline.

The public, thoroughly angered by his attack on his wife, gave little thought to buying or reading anything other than pamphlets, lampoons, and caricatures on this disgraceful affair. There was no market for fine poetry throughout England and Scotland in 1820. Keats had written to Brown in June: 'My book is coming out with very low hopes, though not spirits, on my part. This shall be my last trial; not succeeding, I shall try what I can do in the apothecary line'. In August he mentioned the subject again to Brown but

in an offhand manner. Already he had begun his
posthumous existence.

CHAPTER THIRTEEN

ITALY AND DEATH: 1821

THE JOURNEY TO ITALY, which the doctors said was imperative, filled Keats with dread. Writing to Taylor on 26th August asking for help in making arrangements, he said: 'I shall endeavour to go, though it be with the sensation of marching up against a Battery'. Taylor and Hessey did not fail him. They bought the copyright of the *Lamia* and *Endymion* volumes for £100 and cancelled the advances made on account of *Endymion*. They arranged a letter of credit in Italy for £150 supposed to be covered by £200 George had promised to send. Since Abbey, in control of John's trust fund, refused to finance any part of the trip to Italy, Taylor and Hessey raised £10 each from five persons, John Percival, poet, Peter De Wint and William Hilton, artists, Joseph Bonsor, and James Rice, John's own friend, all of which was handed to Keats to pay for the voyage.

In addition the Earl Fitzwilliam subscribed £50, Haslam also agreed to supply another £50 for use in Italy. Passage was engaged on the brig *Maria Crowther* sailing from London to Naples in September. Woodhouse wrote promising future assistance and ended his letter with a quotation from the sonnet written by the anonymous donor from Teignmouth:

*God bless you! — Take care of yourself, — if it be only
for your friends' sake. Above all, keep your mind at
ease. There are many who take more than a bro-
therly Interest in your welfare — There is certainly
" — one, whose hand will never scant
From his poor store of fruits all thou canst want."—
            And he is,
            Yours very sincerely
            & affectionately,
                Richd Woodhouse.
Kings Bench Walk Temple Saty. night. Sepr 1820 —*

But who was to go with him on this his last journey? In a letter to his sister on 23rd August he told
her: 'A few days ago I wrote to Mr Brown, asking him
to befriend me with his company to Rome. His answer is not yet come, and I do not know when it will,
not being certain how far he may be from the Post
Office to which my communication is addressed. Let
us hope he will go with me'. On the same day he also
told Haslam: 'I have written to Brown to ask him to
accompany me; and in fact am all but on the Road as
the Physician tells me an english winter would do for
me'. From these letters it is certain that John asked
Brown to go to Rome and no doubt expected an acceptance.

When Brown in 1841 gave Keats's letters to R. M.
Milnes, whom he had urged to be biographer of the
poet, the two letters John sent to Scotland contained

no reference to the invitation. Brown had deleted the letters, skilfully making them appear to be a farewell message. Clearly he had no intention of resuming the position of nurse-companion. He was not a rich man and no doubt he felt he could not stand the expense. There was also the complication of Abby's pregnancy. When Keats died in Rome, however, Brown was inconsolable. His conscience evidently troubled him. In his scant and disappointing sketch of the life of Keats written at Plymouth in 1836 Brown put the matter in the best possible light for himself by stating: 'I contented myself by preparing to follow him in the Spring and not return should he prefer to live there'.

It was Haslam's idea that Severn should accompany Keats. He was the only one of the poet's friends except Brown who was unattached. Brown was away and an unknown quantity. Although he was given only a few days notice Severn did not hesitate. It turned out to be the decision on which his success in life and lasting fame were founded. He could not have known that. He was really taking some risk in giving up his hard won self support as a painter of miniatures. Meanwhile Keats was living where he longed to be, happy in the undivided attention of Fanny and, as to his health, under the watchful eye of Mrs Brawne. In preparation for his voyage he sent Taylor a sort of testamentary paper which said: 'All my estate real and personal consists in the hopes of

P

the sale of books publish'd or unpublish'd'. He wished
that Brown and Taylor should be paid first, adding
'the rest is in nubibus'. He gave a characteristic
Keatsian touch to his testament by requesting Taylor
to pay his tailor a few pounds 'in case it should
shower'.

In mid-August he received a sincere invitation from
Shelley at Pisa asking him to come to Italy and 'take
up his residence' with Shelley and his wife. Keats was
not insensible of the interest and generosity shown
by this friendly letter. He replied: 'If I do not take
advantage of your invitation it will be prevented by a
circumstance I have very much at heart to prophesy'.
The circumstance he referred to, I surmise, was the
hope that Fanny might accompany him to Italy. What
a pity it was he ever left England and the only home
in which he could be content!

Keats moved from Hampstead on 13th September
1820 to Taylor's house in London. There he stayed
until the early morning of the seventeenth when the
brig was to sail. This was necessary in order to complete his business arrangements and to be nearer the
dock where the vessel lay. The *Maria Crowther* of
130 tons burthen was a poor choice for the passage to
Italy. Besides the eating saloon, she had only one
cabin in which both the captain and passengers (possibly the mate also) had to live when below deck. It
contained six berths arranged in tiers, one tier for the

officers, one for Severn and Keats and the remaining
tier, with a curtain, for the two lady passengers. As
it turned out on the voyage, the *Maria Crowther* was
insecurely protected against the rage of the sea and
badly provisioned.

In the chilly twilight of Sunday morning 17th September, there gathered at the London dock Keats,
Haslam, Woodhouse, Taylor, Williams (young apprentice employed by Taylor), Severn and Severn's
brother Tom. Mrs Pigeon was already aboard the
brig disposing of her belongings. Miss Cotterell, the
other woman passenger, was to join the ship at Gravesend where outbound vessels always stopped to drop
river pilot, clear customs and settle port dues. Haslam and Woodhouse were going down river as far as
Gravesend. Severn had experienced a distressing encounter with his father on leaving home and had left
behind his passport. His father, opposing his going,
had knocked him down. Haslam volunteered to send
the passport to Gravesend. When Haslam and Woodhouse left Keats and Severn to return to London,
Woodhouse took with him a lock cut from the head
of his beloved poet.

Keats had been calm throughout the bustle of preparation. The river air invigorated him and he seemed
to take an interest in the novelty of his situation. During the night of 17th to 18th September a smack
from Dundee with Charles Brown on board glided

into the river and anchored, unrecognised, within speaking distance of the *Maria Crowther*. The next day the Captain, Thomas Walsh, whom Severn described as a most obliging 'good fellow,' decided to go ashore to buy additional supplies for the voyage. Severn went with him to get apples and sundries for Keats. The missing passport arrived in the afternoon sent by their 'oak friend' Haslam. Miss Cotterell had come aboard meantime and the brig was now ready to put to sea.

Haslam had asked Severn to write all the experiences of the journey. On 19th September off Margate, Severn wrote the first of his many letters. 'We are going on most delightfully,' he said, 'the second Lady has joined us – and it is a most singular coincidence – that she is labouring under the very same complaint as Keats – the same symptons – and the same manner of cure. One very good hope is – we find sick people insisting and quarelling about being worse than each other.' In spite of the 'core of disease' in him which he mentioned in a letter written to Brown in September, John must have had vital endurance to stand the close quarters and monotony of the long voyage to Naples. The *Maria Crowther* was held two weeks in the English Channel by calms or adverse winds. Severn and he landed in Portsmouth on Thursday 28th September and went over to Bedhampton, seven miles distant, to call on the Snooks who told them Brown was visiting old Mr Dilke at Chichester. The Snooks were surprised at the cheerful demeanor of Keats and amused by his lively dislike of Mrs Pigeon who had become the pest of the voyage.

After he returned on board next morning he sat down to write a letter to Brown, the only person to whom he could speak freely about Fanny. In his sad letter he said:

> *If my spirits seem too low you may in some degree impute it to our having been at sea a fortnight without making any way. I was very disappointed at not meeting you at bedhampton, and am very provoked at the thought of you being at Chichester today. I should have delighted in setting off for London for the sensation merely – for what should I do there? I could not leave my lungs or stomach or other worse things behind me. . . . I think without my mentioning it for my sake you would be a friend to Miss Brawne when I am dead. . . . I seldom think of my Brother and Sister – in america. The thought of leaving Miss Brawne is beyond everything horrible – the sense of darkness coming over me – I eternally see her figure eternally vanishing.*

After five dreary weeks the vessel reached the Bay of Naples. A typhus epidemic in London of which they were unaware made it necessary to detain the brig in quarantine for ten days. But chance gave a redeeming touch of *opéra bouffe* to their extended stay on board that provided them with amusement and at the same time made them uncomfortable. An English fleet was anchored in the Bay of Naples. When the *Maria Crowther* sailed in, the Admiral of the fleet, seeing the Union Jack at the brig's masthead, sent Lieutenant Sullivan with six men to make enquiries. They all came aboard and were held prisoners in quarantine. Miss Cotterell, who also had been sent to Italy for her health, came to visit her brother Charles in Naples. He arrived to see his sister and got caught also. The addition of these guests, however, and the good food and wine they were able to have brought on board, made the delay in quarantine a merrier interlude than it otherwise might have been.

Notwithstanding his 'posthumous' feeling, Keats was keenly alive to the beauties of Naples harbour. Vesuvius with its smoke clouds continually changing to a golden glow, the blue water in the Bay of Naples, the mountains of Sorrento, seemingly made of lapis lazuli, and Naples with her terraced gardens and vineyards upon the slopes of the Appenines made a panorama that aroused the artist in Keats and brought relief to his mind. He wrote a letter to Mrs Brawne from quarantine telling her:

The sea air has been beneficial to me about to as great an extent as equally weather and bad accommodations and provisions has done harm – So I am

about as I was — Give my Love to Fanny and tell her,
if I were well there is enough in this Port of Naples
to fill a quire of Paper — but it looks like a dream —
every man who can row his boat and walk and talk
seems a different being from myself. I do not feel in
the world. It has been unfortunate for me that one
of the Passengers is a young Lady in a Consumption
— her imprudence has vexed me very much — the
knowledge of her complaint — the flushings in her
face, all her bad symptoms have preyed upon me —
they would have done so had I been in good health.

He added to the letter a postcript, the last message
he ever wrote to the girl he so deeply loved — 'Goodbye Fanny. God bless you'.

Freed at last on 31st October they landed. Keats
was depressed by the dirt, smells and clamour of
Naples which had appeared so romantic when viewed
from their quarantine anchorage. He whispered to
Severn: 'We'll go on to Rome for I know I shall not
last long and it would make me die in anguish if I
thought I was to be buried among these people'.
Shelley had written a letter to Naples, again urging
his coming to Pisa. Keats had neither desire nor ability to accept. However well intentioned Shelley may
have been, it was a singularly inept idea that he announced to Mrs Hunt: 'I intend to be the physician
both of Keats's body and his soul, to keep the one
warm and to teach the other Greek and Spanish'.

Severn and Keats left Naples for Rome probably on 5th November. Travel by carriage was slow. Severn seems to have walked beside it most of the way. The new scenes were novel and exciting to him but to Keats, wretchedly ill, the journey was unending. He became very listless, Severn said, and was not 'even relatively happy except when an unusually fine prospect opened before us, or the breeze bore to us exquisite hill fragrances or breaths from the distant blue seas, and particularly when I literally filled the little carriage with flowers. He never tired of these, and they gave him almost fantastic pleasure that was at times akin to a strange joy'. Nine days or more had passed before they were able to enter Rome by the Lateran Gate and made their way to the Piazza di Spagna where Dr Clark lived, under whose care Keats was to be. The Piazza di Spagna formed the heart of the English colony at Rome. In its centre was a fountain designed by Bernini in the shape of a galley. On one side a broad flight of steps led to Santa Trinita dei Monti on the Pincian Hill above. These steps served as the short route from the fashionable parade of the hill to the Corso, the main street of Rome. In a house to the right of the steps the doctor had found rooms facing the steps.

Dr Clark's cheerful personality pleased Keats. For a time he seemed to improve. The imposing beauty of Rome, ancient capital of a world gone by, did not fail to make a deep impression on his imagination. He seemed to revive as of old, Severn thought. A feeling of hope came over him; the spirit of the place aroused him. He talked of making good as a poet, he said, 'mostly on account of his friends'. And Severn has recorded the effect on himself of Rome due to the spirit of Keats.

Rome, the real *Rome would never have become a joy to me – not at any rate for a very long time, and even then with difficulty and at best obscurely – had it not been for Keats's talk with me about the Greek Spirit – the Religion of the Beautiful, the Religion of Joy.*

It was to Brown that Keats sent on 30th November from Rome the last letter he ever wrote:

I have an habitual feeling of my real life having passed, and that I am leading a posthumous existence. God knows how it would have been . . . If I recover, I will do all in my power to correct the mistakes made during sickness; and if I should not, all my faults will be forgiven . . . Write to George as soon as you receive this, and tell him how I am, as far as you can guess; and also a note to my sister – who walks about my imagination like a ghost – she is so like Tom. I can scarcely bid you goodbye, even in a letter. I always made an awkward bow.
            God bless you!
                  John Keats.

Dr Clark had recommended horseback riding. For a while Keats was well enough to do this. He also walked on the Pincian Hill with Severn or Lieutenant Elton, another consumptive who was alone in Rome. They watched the crowds parading there. The sight of the gay and notorious Princess Paulina Borghese, sister of Napoleon, amused them. Canova had just done his famous reclining statue of her, mostly nude. They went to see the statue which Keats immediately named 'The Aeolian Harp'. The songs of birds, the play of light in the Borghese Gardens, the flowers massed in the fountains everywhere, interested him. Severn during this early period was able to make some contacts to improve his chances of gaining the Royal Academy scholarship which would give him three years of residence in Rome. John was much concerned over the prospect of his friend. He wanted him to paint and go on with his work. He approved of the subject Joseph had chosen – *The Death of Alcibiades* – for his painting. It was later to win his pension for him. While Severn worked Keats studied Italian. But the respite was not long.

On Sunday 10th December he suffered a severe haemorrhage followed by others. He had a high fever. When Dr Clark took ounces of blood from his arm it came thick and black. For two long months he was destined to linger on, clinging to life by a mere thread. There was never again any hope. Keats expressed a

strong desire for music and Severn was able to hire a
pianoforte from their landlady. Dr Clark lent some
volumes of music including Haydn's symphonies.
The fading days of Keats were somewhat soothed by
Severn's playing. His imagination, however, which
served him so well in health, did not help at the end
of his life. He knew too much medicine to be deceived.
He saw himself already buried, feeling the flowers
growing over him, as concrete in thoughts of himself
as he had been in the marvellous images of his great
poems.

All his life Keats had lived in the shadow of an
early death. His temperament enabled him to sense
it. No doubt his use of contrast between life and death
in his poems was for dramatic effect but repeated
references in his letters proved that it was not far
from a morbid thought. He could joke about it, however, as he did to Fanny Brawne: 'I fear I am too prudent for a dying kind of a Lover. Yet, there is a great
difference between going off in warm blood like
Romeo, and making one's exit like a frog in a frost'.
Even on death's bed, when all his bitterness was concentrated on death's delay in coming, his sense of
humour came bubbling up. He directed Severn, who
was writing a letter to his publisher, to 'tell Taylor I
shall soon be in a second edition – in sheets – and
cold press'.

Toward the end of his long day and night vigil,

Severn, fearful that he would fall asleep himself, not wanting Keats to wake up in the dark, fixed a thread from the bottom of a lighted candle to the wick of an unlighted one. When Keats awoke just as the first candle was going out and the thread was conducting the flame to the unlighted one, he cried out, 'Look Severn, Severn! Here's a little fairy lamp-lighter actually lit up the other candle'. It cannot be said of Keats that he missed the crown of immortality from 'fear to follow where airy voices led'.

On 14th February he told Severn 'I want on my grave no name and only the words "Here lies one whose name was writ in water" '. But, even as he was speaking, the spirit of the Bernini Fountain in the centre of the Piazza di Spagna, just underneath his window, answered, telling the world:

> *Little he knew 'twixt his dreaming and sleeping,*
> *The while his sick fancy despaired of his fame,*
> *What glory I held in my loverly keeping;*
> *Listen! my waters will whisper his name.*[27]

Keats talked constantly of dying and longed for the dayspring of another world. Death was crowding him. In spite of it, he remained artist to the end. 'He made me go,' said Severn, 'to see the place where he was to be buried and he expressed pleasure at my description of the locality of the Pyramid of Caius Cestius, about the grass and the many flowers, particularly the innumerable violets, also about a flock of goats and sheep and a young shepherd – all of these intensely interested him.'

During the last few days of his life he became very calm and resigned which made the death summons more terrible. 'Those bright falcon eyes,' known only in joyous intercourse while Keats revelled in books or nature or recited his own poetry, now beamed with an unearthly brightness and a penetrating steadfastness Severn could not face. Keats 'held my hand to the last,' Severn wrote to Brown, 'and he looked up at me until his eyes lost their speculation and dimmed in death. . . . He gasped to me to lift him up – "Severn – I – lift me up, for I am dying. I shall die easy. Don't be frightened. Thank God it has come". I lifted him up in my arms and the phlegm seemed boiling in his throat. This increased until eleven at night when he gradually sank into death, so quiet, that I still thought he slept – but I cannot say more now. I am broken down beyond my strength'.

John Keats died in Rome, Italy, on Friday 23rd February 1821. What his life had been and has come to mean to lovers of poetry was vividly phrased by Elizabeth Barrett Browning in describing him as:

> . . . *The man who never stepped*
> *In gradual progress like another man,*
> *But turning grandly on his central self,*
> *Ensphered himself in twenty perfect years*

And died, not young, (the life of a long life
Distilled to a mere drop, falling like a tear
Upon the world's cold cheek to make it burn
Forever) . . .[28]

EPILOGUE

THE FUNERAL PROCESSION bearing the wasted body
of John Keats left the Piazza di Spagna during the
night between Sunday 25th and Monday 26th February. It was the start of a procession lovers of poetry
have ever since continued to join. Day was breaking
on Monday morning as they buried him. Beside the
open grave stood his friend Severn, Dr Clark, Dr
Wolff (the English Chaplain) and the following persons, attracted by his tragic story: William Ewing,
Richard Westmacott Junior, Henry Parke, Ambrose
Poynter, Dr Luby and an unidentified man named
Henderson.

The grave is in the unused, older part of the burial
ground now known as the Protestant Cemetery, but
in 1821 this spot, where they laid him, was in an open
meadow on the outskirts of Rome, far from the houses
and churches of the faithful, a place set apart for the
graves of non-Catholics whose dead bodies had to be
taken there at night only. It was called the Cemetery
of the Acattolici. A drawing made by James Hakewill
in 1817 shows an unenclosed field with sheep grazing
in the midst of graves near the mouldy Aurelian wall
and close by the Pyramid of Cestius.[29] Though not
like the present well kept shrine, shaded by cypress,

acacia, pine and ilex, to which hundreds of worshippers of Keats and Shelley go each year, it was a beautiful place full of wild flowers and peaceful stillness.

The headstone of his grave perpetuates, however, the obnoxious, long persisting notion that he was killed by adverse criticism. It would naturally have happened, no doubt, that John in his last sickness did suffer bitter regrets, mostly concerning Fanny Brawne and his lost opportunities in life. He probably never thought, certainly never spoke, about the Scottish reviewers. Severn says emphatically that in Rome Keats did not mention them. Brown, who wrote the epitaph, belittled the robust manhood of his friend by ascribing his death to bitterness of heart 'at the malicious power of his enemies'. Brown knew full well that the bitterness with which the heart of Keats was engulfed had to do only with his love for Fanny Brawne because he had received from Naples a letter dated 1st November 1820 telling him so:

> *My dear Brown, I should have had her when I was in health, and I should have remained well. I can bear to die — I cannot bear to leave her. Oh, God! God! God! Everything I have in my trunks that reminds me of her goes through me like a spear. The silk lining she put in my travelling cap scalds my head. My imagination is horribly vivid about her — I see her — I hear her. There is nothing in the world of sufficient interest to divert me from her a moment.*

Resentment against fate had often made Keats downcast but he was too self assured to be overcome by criticism of his writing.

Cowden Clarke, who knew him well, and Fanny Brawne, who loved him, have squelched the notion that Keats was killed by attacks on his poems which, as he well knew, were in reality aimed at the Hunt coterie. Clarke wrote in his *Biographical Notes on Keats*:

> *It is a great mistake; and no friend to the memory of Keats would give currency to the report that his death was attributable to the attacks of the reviewers. The reviewers did not kill him; for his last work was his best. They hurt his heart, it is true; and a man must indeed be obtuse who could be indifferent to the wanton and unprovoked insult with which he was assailed. But he perfectly understood the animus of the organised system of that age.*

At the time the reviews of *Endymion* attempted in 1818 to wither Keats with their noxious winds, he was just back from his tour of Scotland. By then he had adopted the humanistic philosophy of 'negative capability' and was immune to attacks, however virulent. In other words he had gained full control of his writing as the future well proved.

'If I should die,' John wrote intimately to Fanny Brawne after his fatal attack in February 1820, 'I

R

have left no immortal work behind me – nothing to
make my friends proud of my memory – but I have
lov'd the principle of beauty in all things, and if I
had had time I would have made myself remember'd.'
He knew, he told Brown at the time, that the haemorrhage was his 'death warrant'. When the end approached and he realised that he would never be able
to finish all he would like to say, I believe it was
simply noble modesty that made him feel his name
was 'only writ in water'. A better headstone for Keats
is the ancient Pyramid of Caius Cestius, casting as it
does its pointed shadow for a portion of each day
over his grave. It serves as a symbol of that other
pyramid, namely, the fame he built for himself by
the splendour of his genius.

BIRTHPLACE AND FAMILY:
1795-1803

JOHN KEATS was born on the thirty-first day of October 1795, at the Swan and Hoop livery stable, 24 Moorfields Pavement Row, a main highway into the heart of London along which horsemen, wagons and carts made their noisy way. The din of traffic, the cries of knife grinders and pedlars on the busy street were the sounds greeting the infant John in strange contrast to his later worship of stillness.

Standing before the site of the Swan and Hoop (now 85 Moorgate Street) in the much built-up city, one can see today, almost at the corner of Fore Street, only an unimpressive building of three stories. Although it bears a tablet telling of the birth of a poet, the site now advertises more impressively the sale of Worthington's Ale. When the Swan and Hoop existed, it looked out on the Moorfields, an open space of which the only green remnant is the oval park known as Finsbury Circus.

John Jennings, the poet's grandfather, after whom he was named, had developed a prosperous business amounting to over £13,000 at the sign of the Swan and Hoop (said to be in present day values at least £30,000). He also owned an adjacent house or houses on the Row which he let out in tenements. Though there is no record of his origin, at least we know that his wife, Alice Jennings, was born in Lancashire and had lived in the village of Colne, according to Richard Abbey, her fellow townsman, who later became, by her appointment, guardian of the Keats orphans. Three children, two boys and one girl, completed the Jennings family. One of the sons died before maturity, the other, Midgley John Jennings, grew to manhood, was educated at John Clarke's School in Enfield and took part as Lieutenant of Marines in the Royal Navy at the Battle of Camperdown in 1797. The daughter, Frances, when nineteen years old, fell in love with Thomas Keats, head ostler in the stable of her father. She married him in St George's Church, Hanover Square, London, on 9th October 1794.

When Thomas Keats came to work for John Jennings is not known. His employer, however, must have thought well of his head man to allow him to marry his only daughter and leave him in sole charge of his business. Early in 1795 John Jennings retired to Ponders End, a village close to the Enfield highway on the border of Edmonton in Middlesex. The history of Thomas Keats before he arrived at the Swan and Hoop is also unknown. He is supposed to have come from Cornwall near Lands End, according to recollections (in her old age) of his daughter, Fanny, the only surviving member of the family. The name Keats in various spellings was common enough in the southern part of England. Apparently the word is of Scandinavian derivation from 'Kete' meaning bold, courageous, which quite fits the manliness of John Keats, the poet. There is an interesting speculation developed by Colvin that Thomas Keats and John Jennings, who may himself have come from Cornwall where the name is familiar, were related and thus the younger gained the confidence of the elder man. To support this there was a Thomas Keast born in Cornwall in the same year 1768 as Thomas Keats, according to a church register in the parish of St Agnes between Redruth and Newquay. The supposition is that the more familiar spelling of Keats would likely have been adopted on his coming to London. The pronunciation is nearly the same.

Whatever his past had been Thomas Keats and his wife, Frances, were a happy, devoted couple. They began their married life at the Swan and Hoop and their first child, John, was born there a year after their marriage. He was christened at St Botolph's Church, Bishopsgate on 18th December 1795. A second son, George, followed on 28th February 1797, Thomas on 18th November 1799; a fourth son (who died in infancy) in April 1801, and their last child Frances Mary on 3rd June 1803. Meantime with prosperity and an increasing family, the parents had moved to Craven Street, City Road, about three-quarters of a mile north of the stable, almost in the open country. The new abode, also, was near Charles Square, a quiet, green place with trees, where the children could be taken to play. Some of the old houses on Craven Street still exist but which was occupied by the Keats family is not known.

The custom among well-to-do English families of taking sons away from home influence at an early age and placing them in a boarding school must have seemed to Thomas Keats a logical consequence of having sons to bring up. His wife's brothers had gone to the Clarke school in Enfield. Although ambition for their sons led Thomas and Frances, it is said, to consider sending them to the more famous school of Harrow on the Hill, it was decided, perhaps on John Jennings' conservative advice, that John Clarke's school would do. Both John and George were taken to Enfield by their parents in the late summer of 1803, the year of their sister's birth. The youngest brother Tom was to join them at school a little later. George had grown taller than his older brother and the Clarke family thought him the elder, causing Charles Cowden Clarke, the son, to describe John incorrectly in his *Recollections of Writers* as 'the youngest individual in a corporation of between sixty and seventy youngsters – one of the little fellows who had not wholly emerged from the child's costume'. John was nearly eight years old and George six and a half at the time they entered the Clarke School.

John Clarke and his wife found Thomas and Frances Keats alert and respectable parents interested in the welfare and care of their sons. They were welcomed from time to time, driving over to Enfield in their gig from the Craven Street house. They always made a good impression on the Clarke family. Gossip retailed by Abbey to John Taylor in 1827, more than six years after John Keats's death, attacking the poet's father, mother and grandfather, is unconfirmed from any other source and may be brushed aside, I think, as the spiteful opinion of a stubborn old man who formerly, in 1810, had been appointed guardian of the Keats children. Cowden Clarke who knew the Jennings as well as the Keats family, and especially admired Lieutenant Midgley John, wrote to R. M. Milnes, first biographer of the poet:

> To say that John Keats's family were 'respectable,' in the common acceptance of the term, would be an impertinence . . . they were, indeed all of them that I remember, estimable.

At the end of 1803 not a cloud cast its threatening shadow over the prospects and relationship of Thomas Keats and his wife. The year 1804 began well, too, but it did not continue so. One Sunday afternoon or evening in April of that year Thomas Keats rode alone to meet a sudden, tragic death. He had gone to

Southgate, a small village at the Southern entrance to
Enfield Chase. On his return, when riding along City
Road on his way to the stable, his horse apparently
stumbled and threw him against an iron fence opposite the Wesley Chapel, crushing his skull. The night-
watchman making his rounds found him lying un-
conscious. Well known in the neighbourhood, he was
removed to a nearby house and his wife sent for. He
could not speak to her and died at eight o'clock in the
morning of the next day, 17th April, without regain-
ing consciousness.

The shock and loss were too great to be safely
borne by his wife. No doubt due to her emotional
nature and inexperience, she felt herself incapable of
managing the livery stable. Her father who was destined to die early in the following year, 1805, may
have been too incapacitated to help her by taking on
again the management of the business. It is not known
how one William Rawlings came into her life. Without a vestige of judgment, patience or self restraint,
Frances Keats consoled herself by marrying Rawlings
on 27th June 1804 just two months after her first husband's death. In what must have been a daze, she had
the ceremony performed in the same church as her
first marriage. It has happened elsewhere in life's experience, and may have been true in this case, that
Frances Keats was demented temporarily by the
shock of sudden death, depriving her of the steady-

ing influence of a well balanced husband. The marriage to Rawlings was like a conjuror's trick — a hocus pocus which affected materially the prospects of her children, her own happiness and her parents' pride and peace of mind. Mrs Jennings, who disapproved of the marriage, took the children to Ponders End. Frances disillusioned within the year, returned to her children at her mother's house. From Ponders End Mrs Jennings moved, after her husband's death to Church Street, Edmonton.

John Jennings made his will on 1st February 1805, and died the following April. Evidently he had parted with title to the stable after Thomas Keats married Frances for it was not listed as an asset in his will. By his daughter's re-marriage, her husband, under the then existing law in England, took title to any property she had. Not a penny from the stable came to her children so far as is known. In addition to misfortune resulting from the rash and inconsiderate act of Frances Keats Rawlings, the will of her father did not fully distribute all of his property, a detail which put the estate under jurisdiction of the Chancery Court where, in part, it remained until his granddaughter, Fanny, came of age in 1824. Much of John's friction with Abbey and the excuse for withholding income, had to do with questions alleged to be unsettled in Chancery. The only benefit, if indeed there was any, of the Keats children's being left alone in the world, was mentioned by John in a letter to his friend Benjamin Bailey in June 1818:

My Love for my brothers from the early loss of our parents and from even earlier Misfortune has grown into a[n] affection 'passing the Love of Women' —

PERSONAL APPEARANCE OF JOHN KEATS

LIKE HIS FATHER, who is said to have come up to London from the West Country, John Keats had a russet colouring. Amy Lowell, herself a poet, who searched the skies for facts concerning Keats and was exhaustive in her search, has attested by examination the colour of his hair.

> There are locks of Keats's hair in the Dilke, Morgan and Day collections. The Morgan Library possesses the least faded of these and the colour is simply marvellous. Such a red I think I never saw before; no word can exactly describe it. It is lighter than the shade known as Titian red and yet with no suggestion of the hue called carrot. A red sunset comes nearer to the colour. The man with such glorious hair must have been striking in the extreme.

According to his Oxford friend, Benjamin Bailey, 'If you placed your hand upon his head the curls fell around it like a rich plumage'.

Though not more than an inch over five feet Keats actually seemed taller. His erect attitude, broad shoulders, well proportioned body, backward toss of head and dauntless expression, all contributed to give this effect. There are varying accounts of his eyes and features. The impact of his personality on his friends is apparent from their romantic descriptions. Joseph Severn spoke of 'the wine-like lustre of his eyes, just those of certain birds which always face the sun' and in another place 'they were like the hazel eyes of a wild gypsy maid in colour, set in the face of a young God'. 'His eyes,' said Robert Haydon, 'had an inward look perfectly divine like a Delphian priestess who had visions . . . [He] was the only man I ever met who seemed and looked conscious of a high calling except Wordsworth.' And Leigh Hunt wrote after Keats's death '[He] had a face in which energy and sensibility were remarkably mixed up, an eager power checked and made patient by ill health . . . At the recital of a noble action or a beautiful thought [his eyes] would suffuse with tears and his mouth trembled. In this there was ill health as well as imagination for he did not like these betrayals of emotion and he had great personal as well as moral courage'.

Mrs B. W. Proctor (wife of Barry Cornwall) described Keats for R. M. Milnes: 'I never saw him but twice but his countenance lives in my mind as one of singular beauty and brightness – it had an expression as if he had been looking on some glorious sight'.

Benjamin Bailey sent his reminiscences from Ceylon to R. M. Milnes: 'The form of his head was like that of a Greek statue . . . and he realised to my mind the youthful Apollo more than any head of any living man whom I have known', and even Felton Mathew, not a faithful friend, made his florid gesture of obeisance: 'A painter or a sculptor might have taken him for a study after the Greek masters and have given him "a station like the herald Mercury, new lighted on some heaven-kissing hill" '.

Fortunately there exists a true likeness of the poet in a life mask made by Haydon. The strength and beauty there represented was verified as authentic by his sister Fanny. She described it as a 'perfect copy of the features of my dear brother'. He was 'Homer-browed'; nose and cheek bones prominent; mouth determined and chin of character; the likeness of a man strong, sensitive and deeply reflective of things seen and unseen. Severn drew or painted Keats in health at least twice and made at Rome a remarkable sketch of his wasted, dying face.

The first known portrait of the poet is the drawing (now in the Victoria and Albert Museum) made at 76 Cheapside by Severn about the end of 1816 when Cowden Clarke was present. John expressed satisfaction with a likeness of himself sent to his sister in June 1819, calling it 'a very capital profile done by Brown' (now at Hampstead).

There are sketches by Charles Brown, Haydon, Mrs Leigh Hunt, also posthumous pictures by Severn, William Hilton and others as well as later busts and medallions. No portrayal, however, is accurate that does not tell of his gaiety and strong sense of humour. As to that Cowden Clarke said: 'His sense of humour, with the power of transmitting by imitation, was both vivid and irresistibly amusing'.

THE RELIGION OF KEATS

OF HIS IDEAS on personal survival there is, first of all, the little poem written at Edmonton as a youth of nineteen, which contained his first known comments on death:

> *Can death be sleep, when life is but a dream,*
> *And scenes of bliss pass as a phantom by?*
> *The transient pleasures as a vision seem,*
> *And yet we think the greatest pain's to die.*
>
> *How strange it is that man on earth should roam,*
> *And lead a life of woe, but not forsake*
> *His rugged path; nor dare he view alone*
> *His future doom which is but to awake.*

The same view was held by him when he wrote *Sleep and Poetry* just after he abandoned his career in medicine:

> *Stop and consider! life is but a day;*
> *A fragile dew-drop on its perilous way*
> *From a tree's summit; a poor Indian's sleep*
> *While his boat hastens to the monstrous steep*
> *Of Montmorenci.*

In November 1817 he ventured an opinion on life after death in a letter to Bailey from the Fox and Hounds Inn at Burford Bridge where he was finishing

Endymion. A life of 'Sensations,' he said, is 'a shadow
of reality to come – and this consideration has further
convinced me – for it has come as auxiliary to another
favourite speculation of mine, – that we shall enjoy
ourselves hereafter by having what we called happiness on Earth repeated in a finer tone'.

After Tom's death he gave George in January 1819
a more mature philosophy:

> *I have scarce a doubt of immortality of some nature*
> *of [for or] other – neither had Tom. . . . sometimes*
> *I fancy an immense separation, and sometimes, as*
> *at present, a direct communication of Spirit with*
> *you. That will be one of the grandeurs of immor-*
> *tality – There will be space and consequently the*
> *only commerce between spirits will be by their in-*
> *telligence of each other – when they will completely*
> *understand each other – While we in this world*
> *merely comp[r]ehend each other in different de-*
> *grees – the higher the degree of good so higher is*
> *our Love and friendship.*

Sitting at Tom's bedside John had known only too
well Tom's struggle to hold on to life. What his eyes
then witnessed he described as the anguish of Apollo,
and with the same meaning, in the last verses of
Hyperion before he abandoned the poem in the
spring of 1819:

> *Soon wild commotions shook him, and made flush*
> *All the immortal fairness of his limbs;*

> *Most like the struggle at the gate of death;*
> *Or liker still to one who should take leave*
> *Of pale immortal death, and with a pang*
> *As hot as death's is chill, with fierce convulse*
> *Die into life:*

At nineteen Keats had thought man's doom is 'but to awake'. I believe his faith at the age of twenty-four in 1819 was the same. He had not forgotten the tolerant and Christian upbringing of the Clarke School.

Influenced by Shelley, perhaps, who delighted in shocking with his scepticism, he tried his hand at writing a sonnet against what he called 'Vulgar Superstition'. It must have been rather a stunt because his brother Tom and Henry Stephens said he wrote it in fifteen minutes. Some church bells, calling people to prayers and 'other gloominess,' were ringing. The sextet of the sonnet sounds rather bombastic:

> *Still, still they toll, and I should feel a damp –*
> *A chill as from a tomb, did I not know*
> *That they are dying like an outburnt lamp;*
> *That 'tis their sighing, wailing ere they go*
> *Into oblivion; –*

Keats was not concerned with Christian devotion day by day but Cowden Clarke, who knew his nature well and his manner of thinking better than anybody else, has written:

s

Every day, Keats once said, was Sabbath to him, as it is to every grateful mind. Sunday was, indeed, Keats's 'day of rest' and I may add, too, of untainted mirth and gladness, as I believe, too, of unprofessing, unostentatious gratitude.

The last words ever spoken by Keats, according to Severn, were words of gratitude and submission. They were 'Thank God it has come'.

FAME: THE FIRST HUNDRED YEARS

EVEN THOUGH he may have had poetical longing to vanish into the forest with the nightingale, Keats took the precaution to announce in January 1818 the manner in which he wished to return from the forest:

When I am through the old oak forest gone
Let me not wander in a barren dream
But when I am consumed with the Fire
Give me new Phoenix-wings to fly at my desire

Familiar with ancient Eastern folk lore concerning that fabulous bird, the phoenix, he knew well the legend—tired of old age in the Arabian desert, it had built a funeral pyre and was burned to ashes. Out of the ashes it arose fresh and young again.

Beset with a craving for posthumous fame, John before he reached his twenty-first birthday had drawn a detailed picture which he sent to George from Margate in August 1816:

What, though I leave this dull, and earthly mould,
Yet, shall my spirit, lofty converse hold
With after times – The Patriot shall feel
My stern alarum, and unsheath his steel:
Or in the senate thunder out my Numbers,
To startle Princes from their easy slumbers.

The Sage will mingle with each moral Theme
My happy thoughts, sententious: he will teem
With lofty Periods, when my Verses fire him,
And then I'll stoop from Heaven, to inspire him.

In this jocular account he was more concerned with
the survival of his poetry than of himself. To have his
poems remain ever young and fresh like the phoenix,
was clearly the immortality he desired. Poesy, he
once said, is 'the supreme of power. 'Tis Might half
slumb'ring on its own right arm'.

Shelley was probably the first person of literary
distinction to appreciate the great gifts of Keats. In
the pocket of the jacket on his body washed ashore
after his drowning, was found the 1820 volume of
Keats's poems folded back as if he had just been reading it before death came to him. Shortly before his
own tragic ending in the Gulf of Spezia, he pro-
claimed in his great eulogy, like the blast of a trum-
pet, the intermingling of his friend with nature and
the welcome awaiting him in another world:

'Tis Death is dead, not he:
Mourn not for Adonais.— Thou young Dawn,
Turn all thy dew to splendour, for from thee
The spirit thou lamentest is not gone!
Ye caverns and ye forests, cease to moan!
Cease, ye faint flowers and fountains! and thou Air,
Which like a mourning veil thy scarf hadst thrown
O'er the abandoned Earth, now leave it bare
Even to the joyous stars which smile on its despair!

He is made one with Nature: There is heard
His voice in all her music, from the moan
Of thunder, to the song of night's sweet bird.
He is a presence to be felt and known
In darkness and in light, from herb and stone,
Spreading itself where'er that Power may move
Which has withdrawn his being to its own,
Which wields the world with neverwearied love,
Sustains it from beneath, and kindles it above.

The inheritors of unfulfilled renown
Rose from their thrones, built beyond mortal
      thought,
Far in the unapparent. Chatterton
Rose pale, — his solemn agony had not
Yet faded from him; Sidney, as he fought
And as he fell and as he lived and loved
Sublimely mild, a spirit without spot,
Arose; and Lucan, by his death approved;
Oblivion as they rose shrank like a thing reproved.

And many more, whose names on earth are dark,
But whose transmitted effluence cannot die
So long as fire outlives the parent spark,
Rose, robed in dazzling immortality.
Thou art become as one of us, they cry,
It was for thee yon kingless sphere has long
Swung blind in unascended majesty,
Silent alone amid an heaven of song.
Assume thy winged throne, thou Vesper of our
      throng!

In 1822 Shelley's poetry remained as neglected as
that of Keats. *Adonais* was little known. It was re-
published in 1829 through the efforts of Arthur Hal-
lam, Tennyson, Richard Monckton Milnes and others
studying at Cambridge University, a group of twelve
young enthusiasts known as the 'Cambridge Apostles'
who had come to know and love the works of both
poets. Indeed Shelley, without intending to, had belittled the fame of his friend by describing him in
Adonais as:

> *A pale flower by some maiden cherished*
> *And fed with true-love tears, instead of dew.*

This was the popular notion of the time, made solid
by Byron's sarcastic lines about Keats:

> *'Tis strange the mind, that very fiery particle*
> *Should let itself be snuffed out by an article.*

Besides Shelley, two other contemporaries of Keats
were well qualified to appraise his poems. Lamb who
admitted he preferred *The Pot of Basil* ('the finest
thing in the volume') to the *Eve of St Agnes, Lamia,
Hyperion,* and the odes; Hazlitt who, many years
older, probably thought John in life an erratic youth,
said in his *Select English Poets,* published in 1824,
that Keats's poems 'displayed extreme tenderness,
beauty, originality and delicacy of feeling'.

Browning, while still a boy of fourteen in 1826, discovered Keats. He continued all his life to read him. As late as 1877 he called Milton and Keats 'the super-human poet-pair'. It is probable too that Tennyson, before entering Cambridge in 1828, had read the 1820 volume because on publication of his first poems in 1830 the reviewers at once noticed the kinship between him and Keats. Walter Savage Landor composed in 1828 a poem to honour Keats. Later in his *Imaginary Conversations* he said: 'I acknowledge there are many wild thoughts in Keats and there are expressions which even outstrip them in extravagance but in none of our poets, with the sole exception of Shakespeare, do we find so many phrases so happy in their boldness'. Even Thackeray who limited his poetry to comic situations early recognized the homage due — a homage he would not give, he said, 'to the whole tribe of humorists'.

Tennyson quickly sensed the perfection of the 'wild and wonderful lines' of Keats:

With his high spiritual vision [he] would have been, if he had lived, the greatest of us. There is something magic and of the innermost soul of poetry in almost everything he wrote.

Ranking him above Wordsworth and Shelley but below 'the great sage poets' who were great thinkers

and great artists too, like Aeschylus, Shakespeare,
Dante and Goethe, Tennyson added:

Keats is wonderful . . . never wild and wilful but al-
ways had a definite intention. At the same time he
was daimonisch. *He was a livery stable keeper's son*
— I don't know where he got it except from heaven.

Most of the Victorian writers except Hazlitt, Lamb,
Hood, Landor, Tennyson, Browning and Thackeray
were born after the death of Keats. They probably
became acquainted with his poetry through the *Life,*
Letters and Literary Remains of John Keats by
Richard Monckton Milnes (afterwards Lord Houghton) published in London in 1848. Although the
Milnes biography is carelessly edited particularly in
the texts and quotations supplied by friends of Keats
whom he consulted, it is the book that revived interest in the life and works of the poet.

Much is owed to Milnes, who was induced by Landor to write the life of Keats. He was one of the most
remarkable men of his time, a brilliant and compelling personality. He had a real love and appreciation
of poetry and was a generous benefactor of literary
men. Had he concentrated on poetry he might have
won a high place in literature. He was mentioned for
the position of Poet Laureate. Tennyson rapidly
eclipsed him. It was Milnes, in fact, who recommended Tennyson for the Laureateship. In London

society he was famous for a generation. At his dinner table all men of eminence in art or politics foregathered. His nicknames – in the banter of London clubs – 'Cook of the Evening,' 'London Assurance,' 'Bird of Paradox,' indicate his peculiar quality as presider over those feasts of wit and fancy.

While Keats was still a medical student in London he recorded gratefully his indebtedness to his predecessors in poetry:

> *How many bards gild the lapses of time!*
> *A few of them have ever been the food*
> *Of my delighted fancy, – I could brood*
> *Over their beauties, earthly, or sublime:*
> *And often, when I sit me down to rhyme,*
> *These will in throngs before my mind intrude:*

In like manner Keats inspired the Victorian poets. Tennyson, Landor, Hood (brother-in-law of Reynolds), Browning, Matthew Arnold, Rosetti, Swinburne, Burne-Jones, Meredith, R. H. Horne, Oscar Wilde and Robert Bridges were in varying degrees indebted to Keats. His imagination opened up vistas of progress to their minds, to be later expressed in pictorial words and made up compounds taken from his writings.

Matthew Arnold was at once one of his greatest critics and stoutest admirers. Appreciating what he called 'natural magic' in Keats he borrowed liberally from the odes. 'No one else in English poetry, save Shakespeare,' he said, 'has in expression quite the fascinating felicity of Keats, his perfection of loveliness.' He was much concerned with the young poet's morals and found his love exuberance for Fanny Brawne excessive. On the whole Keats fared well. His humble wish to be among England's recognised poets called forth Arnold's famous reply: 'He is – he is with Shakespeare.' Arnold had the reputation of being one of the severest critics of mankind, which caused a friend of his on hearing of his death to say: 'Poor Arnold. He won't like God'.

The Victorians known as the 'Pre-Raphaelite Brotherhood' adopted Keats as one of themselves. Rossetti liked his 'flawless gifts' and called *Endymion* 'a magic toy fit for the childhood of a divine poet'. Swinburne wrote 'no countryman of ours since Keats has made . . . words fall into such faultless folds and forms of harmonious line'. 'What I most love,' chuckled Sir Edward Burne-Jones, 'are the little things in Keats that make me tingle every time I say them.' And other Victorian painters drew subjects for their pictures, as Burne-Jones did, from the poems. *The Eve of St Agnes, Isabella, La Belle Dame Sans Merci* and *Endymion* were each used more than once and the *Ode on a Grecian Urn* at least once. 'Surely,' said G. H. Ford – 'If a Keats had not existed, the Victorians would have had to invent one.'

Meanwhile in America the reading public welcomed the poetry of Keats as soon or sooner than English readers did. At Brook Farm (a colony of cultural faddists) in Massachusetts, according to Van Wyck Brooks, embryo poets 'plucked weeds to the rhythms of Keats'. James Russell Lowell, who enjoyed pitching hay in the meadows of Elmwood as much as being a popular author, had early planned to write a life of Keats, a project his kinswoman carried out almost a century later. Dr Oliver Wendell Holmes lectured on Keats's poetry, especially praising *Lamia;* and Charles Eliot Norton, one of the first lovers of his fame, restored order to and planted myrtle and violets at his grave in Rome.

Although Keats had only a small following in the nineteenth century it was a select one. But it did not include by any means all it should have even among educated people. The tide soon turned. The first memorial ever erected to the fame of Keats was a bust made by Anne Whitney. It was placed in the parish church of St John at Hampstead in 1894 with this inscription:

> *To the eternal memory of John Keats*
> *This monument is erected by Americans.*

After its public unveiling, presided over by Edmond Gosse, and an advertised showing of Keats relics and manuscripts in 1895, arranged by Sir Charles

Dilke (grandson of the friend and contemporary of
the poet), to celebrate the hundredth anniversary of
his birth, general interest in the poems and in his
personal tragedy increased rapidly and is still mount-
ing.

> *If one English poet might be recalled today from*
> *the dead to continue the work he left unfinished on*
> *earth [wrote Robert Bridges in 1895] it is probable*
> *the Crown of his country's desire would be set on*
> *the head of John Keats.*[30]

Modern critics have vied with one another in re-
storing to his brow the laurels that Keats in jest at
Hunt's had once placed there himself, afterwards
apologising in an *Ode to Apollo* for the affront. H. W.
Garrod professor of poetry at Oxford University appraised the 1820 volume of the poems in burning
words:

> *The more I read it, the more disposed am I to think*
> *this book to be, of all the world's books, upon the*
> *whole the most marvellous. It was finished before*
> *Keats had completed his twenty-fifth year; and there*
> *is nothing in it which is not in its kind a masterpiece.*
> *Isabella, which Lamb thought the 'finest thing' in*
> *the volume, was written when Keats was not yet*
> *twenty-three. He had just turned twenty-three*
> *when he made the first draft of* Hyperion. *Of the*
> *longer pieces the most perfect is, I think,* The Eve

of St Agnes . . . more fully there than elsewhere we feel what Matthew Arnold means when he speaks of Keats's 'perfection of Loveliness'. Yet even St Agnes must yield to the odes.

Lord Gorell has summed up present day paradoxes of this poet. They are, first, the extent of his elevation from obscurity to a realm beyond anything but uncritical adoration; secondly, this elevation has been heightened in the twentieth century, yet his spirit is alien to the spirit of this century.

To say of him that he was a fine artist and a fine poet merely describes his technical perfection. But Keats, a true poet, 'becomes something more,' so wrote Arthur Lynch in the 'Memorial Volume' of 1921, 'he seems the mind the most finely touched, the most deeply inspired by the celestial meaning, of all in the range of literature'.

Till the Future dares
Forget the Past, his fate and fame shall be
An echo and a light unto eternity.

THE END

BIBLIOGRAPHY

A complete list of manuscript material, covering many pages, for the study of Keats's life and poetry is given in *The Evolution of Keats's Poetry* by CLAUDE L. FINNEY (Harvard Press, 1936.)

SELECTED BIBLIOGRAPHY FOR
GENERAL REFERENCE

H. BUXTON FORMAN, editor: *The Poetical Works and Other Writings of John Keats*: library edition in four volumes. (London, 1883.)

M. BUXTON FORMAN, editor: *The Letters of John Keats:* fourth edition. (Oxford, 1952.)

HYDER EDWARD ROLLINS, editor: *The Keats Circle* (letters and papers, 1816-78): two volumes. (Cambridge, 1948). *Keats's Reputation in America to 1848.* (Cambridge, 1946.)

SIR SYDNEY COLVIN: *John Keats* (His Life and Poetry, His Friends, Critics and After Fame). (Scribners, New York, 1917.)

AMY LOWELL: *John Keats.* (H & M, Boston, 1925.)

DOROTHY HEWLETT: *A Life of John Keats.* (H & B, London, 1950.)

RICHARD MONCKTON MILNES (Lord Houghton): *The Life, Letters and Remains of John Keats*: two volumes. (London, 1848.)

CHARLES COWDEN CLARKE: *Recollections of Writers.* (London, 1878.) *The St James Holiday Annual*: for 1875. *The Tatler*: issue of 11th October, 1830.

MARY COWDEN CLARKE: *My Long Life.* (London, 1896.)

MALCOLM ELWIN, editor: *Autobiography of Benjamin Robert Haydon.* (McDonald, London, 1950.)

Sir William Hale-White: *Keats as Doctor and Patient.* (Oxford, 1938.)

C. L. Fletoe: *Memorials of John Flint South.* (London, 1884.)

Marchette Chute: *Shakespeare of London.* (New York, 1949.)

Aubury de Selincourt: *Six Great Englishmen.* (London, 1953.)

J. H. Leigh Hunt: *Lord Byron and Some of his Contemporaries*: two volumes. (Colburn, London, 1828.)

The Autobiography of Leigh Hunt: edited by his eldest son: two volumes.

A. J. B. Erlande: *The Life of John Keats.* (New York, 1929.)

William Sharp: *The Life of Joseph Severn.* (London, 1892.)

H. W. Garrod, editor: *The Poetical Works of John Keats.* (Oxford, 1939.)

E. V. Lucas: *The Colvins and their Friends.* (Methuen, London.)

The Keats Memorial Volume. (John Lane, London, 1921.)

Marie Adami: *Fanny Keats.* (Murray, London, 1937.)

Robert Bridges: *John Keats, a Critical Essay.* (Bullen, London, 1925.)

Donald Parson: *Portraits of Keats.* (World Co, New York, 1954.)

Percy Bysshe Shelley: *Adonais.* (Oxford, 1891.)

A History of Enfield (for subscribers only): compiled by Ford and Hudson. (Enfield, 1873.)

W. J. Loftie: 'Keats at Enfield' in *Poets' Country:* edited by Andrew Lang. (London, 1907.)

History of the Parish Church of Enfield dedicated to St Andrew. (Meyers Brooks & Co, Enfield, [reprinted] 1953.)

T. J. BARRATT, editor: *Annals of Hampstead.* (Black, London, 1812.)

E. F. OPPÉ: *Hampstead, A London Town.* (Hampstead, 1951.)

J. H. PRESTON: *The Story of Hampstead.* (London, 1948.)

GEORGE H. FORD: *Keats and the Victorians.* (Yale, New Haven, 1944.)

CHARLES TENNYSON: *Alfred Tennyson.* (London, 1950.)

WILLIAM HAZLITT: *Lectures on the English Poets.* (T & H, London, 1818.)

JOHN LIVINGSTONE LOWES: *The Road to Xanadu.* (H & M, Boston, 1930.)

SIR CHARLES W. DILKE, Bart, editor: *Papers of a Critic:* (selected from the writings of the Late Charles Wentworth Dilke): two volumes. (London, 1875.)

EDMUND C. BLUNDEN: *Shelley and Keats as They Struck Contemporaries.* (Beaumont, London, 1925.)

Keats's Publisher. (Cape, London, 1936.)

Shelley, A Life Story. (Collins, London, 1946.)

F. W. HAYDON, editor: *Haydon, Correspondence and Table Talk.* (C & W, London, 1896.)

CHARLES BROWN: *Life of John Keats.* (Oxford, 1937.)

ERNEST RAYMOND: *Two Gentlemen of Rome.* (Cassell, London, 1952.)

T

ROBERT GITTINGS: *John Keats: The Living Year.* (Heinemann, London, 1954.)

JOANNA RICHARDSON: *Fanny Brawne.* (London, 1952.)

FRED EDGCUMBE, editor: *Letters of Fanny Brawne to Fanny Keats.* (Oxford, 1936.)

GEORGE L. MARSH, editor: *Poetry and Prose of John Hamilton Reynolds.* (London, 1928.)

KATHARINE M. R. KENYON: *Keats in Winchester.* (Warren and Sons Ltd, Winchester.)

J. MIDDLETON MURRY: *Keats and Shakespeare.* (Oxford, 1925.)
The Mystery of Keats. (Neville, London, 1949.)

M. R. RIDLEY: *Keats's Craftsmanship*: (A Study in Poetic Development). (Oxford, 1933.)

CAROLINE F. E. SPURGEON: *Keats's Shakespeare.* (Oxford, 1928.)

CLARENCE DEWITT THORP: *The Mind of John Keats.* (Oxford, 1926.)

SIR CECIL M. BOWRA: *The Romantic Imagination.* (Harvard, Cambridge, 1949.)

W. W. BEYER: *Keats and the Daemon King.* (Oxford, 1917.)

W. J. BATE: *Negative Capability.* (Harvard, Cambridge, 1937.)

T. S. ELIOT: *The Use of Poetry and the Use of Criticism.* (London, 1933.)

JAMES THORNE: *Handbook to the Environs of London.* (London, 1876.)

NOTES

Note 1. Page 3
A *History of Enfield* (for subscribers only). Compiled by Ford and Hudson. *Enfield 1873* (See Enfield Public Library). *Handbook to the Environs of London* by James Thorne F.S.A. *London 1876.*

Note 2. Page 7
Leigh Hunt referred in his *Autobiography* to the fact that Keats liked helping him with 'A Now, descriptive of a hot day.' The The *Nows* were composed in July or August 1820 but did not appear in *The Indicator* until 28th June 1828.

Note 3. Page 14
Edward Holmes (1797-1859) became a well known writer on music. He was a school friend of Keats and a lifelong friend of Charles Cowden Clarke. He studied music under Vincent Novello, through whom he came to know Charles Lamb and most of the men of letters of his day. With Novello he raised a subscription for Mozart's widow and went to Germany to present it to her in 1828. He taught pianoforte and wrote many articles and books on music including a life of Mozart published in 1845. See D. N. B. Vol. XXVII, page 190.

Note 4. Page 15
Cowden Clark wrote in his *Biographical Notes* that 'Keats was neither an affected nor an ostentatious mannerist; for a more honest minded and honest hearted being never drew breath'. K. C. Vol. II, page 149.

Note 5. Page 15
Keats and the Victorians (a study of his influence and rise to fame —1821-1895) by George H. Ford, *New Haven 1944*, page 27. This book is a well known authority telling of the effect Keats's poetry produced on the Victorians, as described in Appendix IV.

Note 6. Page 20
See A *History of Enfield* (supra), page 286. See also *The History of the Parish Church of Enfield dedicated to St Andrew.* Myers Brooks & Co. Ltd. *Enfield* (reprinted 1953). The Monument to Lady Tiptoft is fully described therein. The Parish

Church of St Andrew was extensively repaired and modernised in the nineteenth century including the laying of a new floor. As to the effect on the poet of Enfield see 'Keats at Enfield' in *Poets' Country*, page 300, *London 1907* (edited by Andrew Lang.)

Note 7. Page 30
John emphasised this remark by adding (without explanation) 'Seven years ago it was not this hand that clench'd itself against Hammond . .' Keats seems to have been proud of his medical knowledge. Clark wrote in *Recollections of Writers:* 'He once talked with me, upon my complaining of stomachic derangement, with a remarkable decision of opinion, describing the functions and actions of the organ with clearness and, as I presume, technical precision of an adult practitioner: casually illustrating the comment, in his characteristic way, with poetical imagery'.

Note 8. Page 32
Shakespeare of London by Marchette Chute, *New York 1949*, gives authentic details of theatres and places in London that Shakespeare and other Elizabethans frequented.

Note 9. Page 34
Memorials of John Flint South by C. L. Fletoe, *London 1884*. John Flint South (1797-1882) became a famous surgeon and was twice chosen president of the Royal College of Surgeons. Sir William Hale-White in *Keats as Doctor and Patient, Oxford Press, 1938*, pages 13 et seq., says: 'The part of Guy's Hospital facing St Thomas's Street looked in 1815 much the same as it does today. In 1814 the Anatomical Department of St Thomas's Hospital had been rebuilt. The new building had a central hall, a museum, a dissecting room and a lecture theatre which, says South, "was one of the most handsome and best fitted rooms for seeing I have ever seen;" there was seating accommodation in it for 290 listeners, one of whom was Keats'. Excellent pictures of Guy's Hospital and St Thomas's Street, as they were in 1815, and of Hammond's house and Keats's cottage at Edmonton are reproduced in *Keats as Doctor and Patient*.

Note 10. Page 35
Henry Stephens (1796-1864) began practice at Redbourn where

Keats saw him on the way to Liverpool with Brown, George and Georgiana in June 1818. He remained at Redbourn for about ten years but his wife and child having died (possibly of cholera) he had removed to London by 1829. Stephens wrote several books, on 'Hernia and other bowel-obstructions,' on 'Cholera' and an original tragedy based on the Saxon period of English history. However his chief fame arose from his invention of the first of the so-called blue-black inks which was known as 'Stephens' writing fluid'. He established a factory at Lambeth, London, prospered, re-married and finally moved to Grove House, Finchley, where he lived the rest of his life. *Life of Henry Stephens* by Matilda Walsh, *Southampton, 1925.* See Encyc. Britt., 11th edition under *Ink.*

Note 11. Page 57
The remarkable details of the early career of Shelley are fully set forth in *Shelley, A Life Story* by Edmund Blunden, *London 1946.*

Note 12. Page 71
Sixteen Self Sketches by G. Bernard Shaw, *London 1949,* page 113.

Note 13. Page 86
Keats's Article was published in *The Champion* under the date of 28th December 1817.

Note 14. Page 107
From *The Cotter's Saturday Night,* stanza XIV. *Complete Poetical Works of Robert Burns, Cambridge 1897.*

Note 15. Page 108
Wordsworth wrote in 1832 a foreword to this sonnet: 'Mosgiel was thus pointed out to me by a young man on top of the coach on the way from Glasgow to Kilmarnock. It is remarkable that, though Burns lived some time here . . . he nowhere adverts to the splendid prospects stretching toward the sea and bounded by the peaks of Arran on one part, which in clear weather he must have daily before his eyes.' *The Complete Poetical Works of William Wordsworth, London 1930,* page 723.

Note 16. Page 150
Sir Charles Dilke, his legatee, was, of course, not the nephew of
Mr Snook, the master baker, ('the boy') but the son of his first
cousin.

Note 17. Page 157
In *Papers of a Critic* (selected from the writings of the late Charles
Wentworth Dilke), Vol I, page 11, Dilke is quoted as having
written: 'It is quite a settled thing between John Keats and Miss
——, God help them. . . . The mother says she cannot prevent it,
and her only hope is that it will go off'.

Note 18. Page 165
Miscellanies. Embracing Nature, Addresses, and Lectures by
Ralph Waldo Emerson, New Edition, *Boston 1876*. See chapter
on 'Languages,' page 32.

Note 19. Page 168
The Complete Works of Samuel Taylor Coleridge, seven vols,
N.Y. 1871. Table Talk Vol. VI, page 412.

Note 20. Page 168
Professor John Livingston Lowes gives an explanation of Coleridge's act in the *Road to Xanadu, Boston 1930,* page 345.

Note 21. Page 168
'The sentiment of the Ode to Fanny proves that Keats composed
it in the spring of 1819 instead of fall. In the spring he felt rebel-
lious against love; but in the fall he surrendered unconditionally
to it. The . . . Ode is an exact and complete interpretation of *La
Belle Dame Sans Merci.* The one expresses a rebellion against the
trammels of love in direct personal style; the other expresses the
same sentiment in objective symbols. Since, in the very nature of
things, direct expression of experience precedes symbolic, the
Ode, I believe, precedes the ballad.' *The Evolution of Keats's
Poetry* by Claude L. Finney, Vol. II, page 593. *Cambridge 1936.*

Note 22. Page 171
The Poems of Emily Dickinson, Boston 1890, page 119.

Note 23. Page 173

> 'My heart, being hungry, feeds on food
> The fat of heart despise.
> Beauty where beauty never stood,
> And sweet where no sweet lies
> I gather to my querulous need,
> Having a growing heart to feed.'

The Harp, Weaver and Other Poems by Edna St Vincent Millay,
New York 1923, page 3.

Note 24. Page 182

This remark by Keats to Reynolds fits Thomas Mann's dictum in
his *Doctor Faustus, N.Y. 1948*, pages 354, 355. 'Elements of illness, working geniuslike are carried over into health? It is not
otherwise . . . genius is a form of vital power deeply experienced
in illness, creating out of illness, through illness creative.' See also
The Infirmities of Genius, by Dr W. R. Bett, *London 1953*, in
which it is claimed that genius and illness have an affinity for each
other.

Note 25. Page 199

Keats-Shelley Journal, Vol. 3 (1954), page 44. That the ode beginning 'Physician Nature,' written with much bitterness, is
properly dated as of the summer of 1820 seems to be proven by
the August 1820 letter to Fanny: 'If my health would bear it, I
could write a poem which I have in my head, which would be a
consolation for people in such a situation as mine. I would show
some one in love as I am, with a person living in liberty as you do.
Shakspeare always sums up matters in the most sovereign manner, Hamlet's heart was full of such misery as mine when he said
to Ophelia, "Go to a Nunnery, go, go!" ' M. B. Forman mentioned
the analogy between the poem and letter. *Letters* (4th edition),
page 503 footnote.

Note 26. Page 199

Ernest Raymond in *Two Gentlemen of Rome, London 1952*, page
144; and Aubury de Selincourt in *Six Great Englishmen, London
1953*, page 177.

Note 27. Page 220
'The Name Writ in Water' (Piazzi di Spagna, Rome)
             The Spirit of the Fountain speaks:
        Yonder's the window my poet would sit in
        While my song murmured of happier days;
        Mine is the water his name has been writ in,
        Sure and immortal my share in his praise. . . .
        Far on the mountain my fountain was fed for him,
        Bringing soft sounds that his nature loved best:
        Sighing of pines that had fain made a bed for him;
        Seafaring rills, on their musical quest: . . .
        Little he knew 'twixt his dreaming and sleeping,
        The while his sick fancy despaired of his fame,
        What glory I held in my loverly keeping:
        Listen! my waters will whisper his name.
Collected Poems (1881-1919) by Robert Underwood Johnson,
New Haven 1920, page 280.

Note 28. Page 222
From the poem *Aurora Leigh. Complete Poetical Works* by Elizabeth Barrett Browning, *Cambridge 1900,* page 268.

Note 29. Page 223
A charming reproduction of Hakewill's drawing is given in *Two
Gentlemen of Rome,* page 86.

Note 30. Page 252
John Keats, a Critical Essay, by Robert Bridges. Privately printed
1895, page 5.

INDEX

Keats, John, date and place of birth, 227; enters John Clarke's school (1803), 3; references to nature and similes traceable to school life, 6, 7, 24; develops fondness for birds, fish, etc, 6; suggests 'Nows' to Hunt, 7; music in his makeup, 12-14, 25; recites *The Eve of St Agnes* to Clarke, 12; description of at school, 14, 15; absence of *juvenilia*, 15; amasses marvellous vocabulary, 15; what he read at school, 16, 17; impressions of visits to Enfield parish church, 17-21; acquiesces in apprenticeship to Hammond, 23, 27; early friendship with Charles Cowden Clarke, 12, 24, 25, 43; his writing of poetry unknown to his brothers or to Clarke, 26; sends verses to Mathew family, 26; death of father, 21; death of mother, 21; death of grandmother, 22, 27; his first attempt at verse, 26; imitates other writers, 27, 37, 38, 41; enters Guy's Hospital, 27; effect of training in Middlesex, 27, 28; where he lived at Guy's, 29, 36, 45; his knowledge and use of medical terms and effect of medical training on his poetry, 29-31; his medical courses, 33; time for poetry at Guy's, 36, 37;

qualifies as surgeon apothecary (1816), 37, 42; supposed to practise at Tottenham, 42; doubts wisdom of abandoning medicine, 42; goes to Margate with Tom, 42; visits Clarke on his return, 45; composes 'Chapman's Homer' sonnet, 45, 46; introduced to Hunt by Clarke, 49; his admiration for Hunt, 49, 50; expresses his 'happy thoughts' in a poem, 50; composes 'I Stood tip-toe' and *Sleep and Poetry*, 51; his later disillusionment, 52; his friendship with Haydon, 53, 56; composes poem in tribute to Wordsworth, Hunt and Haydon, 54; meets Shelley at Vale of Health cottage (1816), 56-58; publishes first book of poems (1817), 58; the effect of hostility of the Olliers, 59; selects Taylor and Hessey as his permanent publishers, 59; celebrates Tom's birthday with a poem (1816), 60; meets Georgiana Augusta Wylie, 61; his friendship with J. H. Reynolds, 49, 63-65; refusing to visit Shelley at Marlow, goes alone to Isle of Wight, 65-67; moves to Margate, 68, to Canterbury, 69; finishes Book I of *Endymion*, goes on holiday to Bo-Peep, 69; his relations with womankind,

HIGH LAND

HAMPSTEAD

WEST HEATH

WEST HEATH

To Spaniards Inn

Upper Flask Inn

VALE OF HE

...OS ROAD

Jack

ROAD

WEST

PLATTS LANE

FORTUNE GREEN

FINCHLEY

LANE

END

WEST END

MILL LANE

ROAD

CHURCH ROW

Parish Church
of St John

WEST END GREEN

WEST END LANE

HAMPSTEAD
IN THE
EARLY NINETEENTH CENTURY

APPROXIMATE LOCATION
OF
STREETS, PATHS AND PLACES
IN
1820

To London

DAT

HIGHSMITH #45230